Keyboard Cash

The Modern Entrepreneur's Dropshipping Playbook

by
William Frye Sr.
AKA:
The Mattress Maverick

Copyright 2024 The Mattress Maverick. All rights reserved.

No part of this book may be reproduced in any form or by any electronic or mechanical means including information storage and retrieval systems, without permission in writing from the author. The only exception is by a reviewer, who may quote short excerpts in a review.

Although the author and publisher have made every effort to ensure that the information in this book was correct at press time, the author and publisher do not assume and hereby disclaim any liability to any party for any loss, damage, or disruption caused by errors or omissions, whether such errors or omissions result from negligence, accident, or any other cause.

This publication is designed to provide accurate and authoritative information with regard to the subject matter covered. It is sold with the understanding that the publisher is not engaged in rendering professional services. If legal advice or other expert assistance is required, the services of a competent professional should be sought.

The fact that an organization or website is referred to in this work as a citation and/or a potential source of further information does not mean that the author or the publisher endorses the information the organization or website may provide or recommendations it may make.

Please remember that Internet websites listed in this work may have changed or disappeared between when this work was written and when it is read.

Table of Contents

Introduction: Navigating the Dropshipping Landscape 1

Chapter 1: Understanding Dropshipping 5
Defining Your Dropshipping Business Model 5
The Pros and Cons of Dropshipping 8
Choosing the Dropshipping Model That Suits You 9

Chapter 2: Setting Up Your Dropshipping Empire 13
Crafting Your Online Presence 13
Selecting the Right Hosting Service 16
Building a User-Friendly Website 17

Chapter 3: Finding Your Niche in the Market 21
Analyzing Market Trends 21
Identifying Profitable Niches 24

Chapter 4: Sourcing Products and Suppliers 28
Where to Look for Reputable Dropshipping Companies 28
Building Relationships with Suppliers 31

Chapter 5: Maximizing Profits Through Pricing 36
Pricing Strategies That Work 36
Competing on Price Without Sacrificing Margins 39

Chapter 6: Crafting the Perfect Sales Funnel 43
Understanding the Customer Journey 44
Creating High-Converting Landing Pages 47
Utilizing Upsells and Cross-sells 47

Chapter 7: The Power of Branding 51
Developing a Memorable Brand Identity 51
Establishing Trust and Credibility 54

Chapter 8: Marketing Your Products.................................58
Mastering Social Media Advertising 58
Harnessing the Power of SEO 61
Email Marketing Do's and Don'ts 62

Chapter 9: Managing Inventory and Orders 66
Streamlining Order Fulfillment 66
Inventory Management Best Practices 69

Chapter 10: Seasonal Sales and Product Trends.........73
Leveraging Seasonality in Your Sales Strategy 73
Predicting and Acting on Product Trends 76

Chapter 11: Customer Service Excellence 80
Understanding the Importance of Customer Satisfaction 80
Handling Complaints and Returns Gracefully.................................. 83

Chapter 12: Scaling Your Business 87
When and How to Scale 87
Hiring and Outsourcing Effectively 90

Chapter 13: Turning Your Keyboard Into Cash............94

Appendix A: Dropshipping Resource Directory.........98

Appendix B: Legal Considerations and Documents.... 101

Appendix C: Case Studies and Success Stories......... 104

Introduction: Navigating the Dropshipping Landscape

The e-commerce revolution has paved the way for enterprising individuals to craft their businesses from the comfort of their homes or local coffee shops. Central to this revolution is the concept of dropshipping—a business model that has democratized the online retail world and allowed countless entrepreneurs to launch their ventures with minimal upfront investment.

With the lure of financial freedom and the promise of being your own boss, it's no wonder that dropshipping has captured the imaginations of many would-be business owners. However, the journey from newcomer to successful online merchant is not without its obstacles and intricacies. This introduction paves the way for understanding the multifaceted environment of dropshipping and sets you up with the fundamental knowledge to chart your course through it.

At its core, dropshipping is a straightforward business model. Retailers sell products to customers, order those sold products from suppliers, and then ship them directly to the buyer's doorstep without ever handling the merchandise themselves. This structure eliminates the need for large capital investments in inventory, making it an attractive option for aspiring entrepreneurs with limited resources.

But don't be mistaken, the simplicity of the model doesn't mean the path is easy. With its growing popularity, the market has become highly competitive. Discerning shoppers, saturated markets, and the logistical challenges of coordinating orders and suppliers add complexity to this seemingly simple business model.

To thrive in the dropshipping world, one must embrace a strategic mindset right from the outset. You'll need to understand the nuts and bolts of setting up an online business, form shrewd marketing tactics, and develop customer service practices that turn one-time shoppers into loyal fans. These early decisions will lay the groundwork for future success.

Many are drawn to dropshipping for its perceived ease and low barrier to entry—yet, without a clear plan and a thorough understanding of how this model works, the business may struggle. We will delve into the imperative first steps of defining your dropshipping business model, discerning the pros and cons, and selecting the right structure for your goals.

Setting up your store is also more than choosing products and a catchy name. It's about crafting a compelling online presence, selecting the right hosting service, and building a user-friendly website—the cornerstones that will help your business stand out in a sea of competitors.

Finding your niche in the market is another critical step. Competition is stiff, so differentiating your business with unique product offerings or tapping into underserved markets can be the difference between a bustling business and a lackluster one.

When it comes to sourcing products and choosing suppliers, developing a keen eye for quality and establishing strong relationships will be vital. Your business will be judged on the products it sells and the reliability of their delivery. When you maximize profits through smart pricing strategies, you ensure that your business not only survives but thrives.

Taking a deep dive into the aspects of crafting the perfect sales funnel will help you convert visitors into customers. By understanding the customer journey, you can create high-converting landing pages and use tactics like upsells and cross-sells to boost your average order value.

The power of branding cannot be overstated in the context of dropshipping. A memorable brand identity and establishing trust are paramount in capturing and retaining customer interest. Your efforts here will set the tone for how the market perceives your business.

Of course, marketing your products effectively will propel your venture forward. Mastery of social media advertising, SEO, and the strategic use of email marketing can skyrocket your brand's visibility and sales.

Once the orders start rolling in, managing inventory and ensuring an efficient order fulfillment process will be critical to maintaining customer satisfaction. Here, we will explore best practices and tools that will help streamline these operations. As your business evolves, so will the challenges of seasonal sales and staying ahead of product trends. Staying agile and responsive to these changes is essential for sustained growth.

Customer service often makes or breaks an e-commerce business. Being adept at handling complaints and processing returns with grace will enhance your reputation and contribute to long-term success.

Eventually, the time will come to scale your business. Knowing when and how to expand, outsource, and hire effectively will be one of the final hurdles in maturing your dropshipping enterprise from a makeshift raft to a sturdy ship ready to sail on the open seas of e-commerce.

This introduction is merely your compass—it can guide you, but the journey ahead rests in your hands. The subsequent chapters will be your map, leading you through the specifics of each critical aspect of building a dropshipping business that is resilient, profitable, and most importantly, yours. Let's set sail into the promising horizon of the dropshipping landscape, where the potential for success only grows with the breadth of your ambition and the depth of your determination.

This industry has changed ALOT since I first started years ago. With the introduction of AI, I decided that it was time for me to start sharing my vast knowledge. Feel free to highlight area's that you want to come back to later. This can be a very fun, exciting and yet challenging journey. Once you've got your first few sales, we'd love to hear from you in our private facebook group.

Chapter 1:
Understanding Dropshipping

In the introductory stage, we sketched a broad overview of the dropshipping business, setting the stage for a deeper dive into its intricate workings. Dropshipping stands as a unique ecommerce model that allows entrepreneurs to operate without holding inventory, transferring customer orders directly to a third party, who then ships the product to the consumer. This introductory chapter lays the foundation, defining the essence of dropshipping, its mechanics, and the critical decision points that await prospective online merchants. Envisioning dropshipping as more than just a means to an end, this chapter will unpack its dynamics, helping you form an unbiased perspective on its advantages and inevitable challenges. Ahead lie the building blocks for constructing your business model; critical considerations that balance flexibility with responsibility and highlight dropshipping's placement within the larger ecommerce ecosystem. We're not just scratching the surface — we're setting the cornerstone for your prospective online empire in the vast digital marketplace.

Defining Your Dropshipping Business Model

As you're venturing deeper into the dropshipping realm, one thing becomes abundantly clear: defining a business model that aligns with your goals, resources, and market understanding is instrumental to your success. Dropshipping, at its core, is about selling products without holding inventory. Nevertheless, how you structure and operate your business can vary significantly, shaping the trajectory of your entrepreneurial journey.

The dropshipping business model involves several key components that you'll need to consider. First and foremost, the product selection process should be done with great care. Choosing products that resonate with your target audience and stand out in the competitive online space is crucial. Finding a balance between demand, profitability, and your personal interest should drive your choices.

Additionally, integrating technology into your operations is a game-changer. You must select e-commerce platforms and tools that offer automation, efficiency, and scalabilities, such as automated order processing and customer relationship management systems, to streamline your business processes.

One of the more nuanced decisions in defining your model is how you want to approach supplier relations. Whether you opt for domestic suppliers for faster shipping times or cast a wider net globally for cost savings, your choice will impact your service quality and profit margins. Upholding supplier relationships built on transparency and reliability is also pivotal for the uninterrupted supply of products.

Another critical aspect is the role of customer service in your business model. Even though you don't handle the inventory, customer satisfaction and loyalty rest upon your shoulders. Establishing a hassle-free communication channel, a clear refund, and return policies, along with diligent follow-through on customer concerns, form the bedrock of a solid dropshipping model.

Further refining your business model involves decision-making about your branding. Will you operate as a generic storefront or invest in branding that can bring about a higher perceived value and customer loyalty? The path you choose can make a big difference in your marketing strategy and overall profitability.

When it comes to pricing, there's no one-size-fits-all strategy. Your approach to pricing needs to factor in your margins, competitor pricing, and the value perception of your products. This will likely evolve as you learn more about your customers' willingness to pay and the competitive landscape.

Moreover, how will you tackle the ongoing management of your dropshipping business? Will you be a one-person show or will you hire a team? Understanding your capacity and when to outsource or bring in more hands is essential for scaling up without compromising the quality of your operation.

Marketing is another pillar of your business model that requires thorough contemplation. You'll need to identify the marketing channels that target your audience most effectively. Whether it's through social media, content marketing, or paid advertising, each channel comes with its own set of rules and potential outcomes.

Furthermore, will your dropshipping business lean heavily on trends or seek evergreen products that have a more consistent selling pattern? The answer influences inventory selection, marketing campaigns, and potentially, the longevity and stability of your sales.

Many entrepreneurs underestimate the power of a sales funnel, but in dropshipping, it's pivotal. Structuring a funnel that not only converts prospects but also retains customers through strategic upselling and cross-selling can amplify your profits considerably.

What's more, as the digital landscape evolves, so should your business model. Stay alert to emerging technologies, e-commerce trends, and changes in consumer behavior to maintain a cutting-edge operation. This adaptive approach may require periodic reassessment and tweaking of your business plan.

Your dropshipping business model should also reflect your risk tolerance. Dropshipping can have slimmer margins than other forms of retail, and your financial framework should accommodate the necessary marketing expenditure, unforeseeable supply chain issues, and other operational risks.

Last but not least, understanding the legalities and ensuring compliance within your dropshipping business cannot be overlooked. This includes everything from tax obligations to intellectual property rights and adherence to e-commerce regulations. Transparent and lawful operations nurture trust and longevity in the business world.

In summary, defining your dropshipping business model is a multifaceted exercise that lays the groundwork for your online venture. It requires a blend of strategic thinking, market research, nuanced decision-making, and regular reassessment to ensure that your approach stays relevant and profitable. As you move through each stage, let your model evolve with the changing tides of the market and technology, holding customer satisfaction and business sustainability at the helm.

The Pros and Cons of Dropshipping

As an enticing option for entrepreneurs looking to break into online retail, dropshipping offers a low overhead pathway; however, there's a balance to strike between its benefits and drawbacks. With dropshipping, individuals gain the advantage of not stocking inventory, which translates to a significant reduction in upfront investment and risk. This model also allows for location flexibility and an expansive product offering without the burden of managing physical stock. On the flip side, these perks come with the challenges of thinner profit margins, as dropshippers often compete with other retailers for the same products. Moreover, there's a relinquished control over inventory and shipping operations, which can lead to longer delivery times and potential issues with product quality—elements that are paramount to customer satisfaction. Resolving these matters typically requires nurturing strong relationships with reliable suppliers and cultivating a sterling customer service strategy to mitigate potential hiccups that can tarnish your brand's reputation.

Choosing the Dropshipping Model That Suits You

As we dissect the concept of dropshipping, it becomes clear that there isn't a one-size-fits-all model. Your dropshipping business should be tailored to your unique strengths, investment capacity, and long-term goals. This section takes you through the various models within dropshipping and helps you pinpoint the one that aligns with your vision.

Firstly, let's consider the general type of products you wish to sell. Some dropshippers focus on trending items, riding the wave of hot products to make quick sales. Others opt for evergreen products that have a steady demand throughout the year. Each has its own set of challenges and benefits; for instance, trending items can offer quick profits but require you to be adept at anticipating and reacting to market trends, while evergreen products afford more stability but may need more effort in branding and customer loyalty.

Another key aspect to consider is whether you want to dropship locally or internationally. Dropshipping to customers in your own country can simplify logistics and customer service, but going global increases your potential market size tenfold. You'll need to weigh up the increased complexity in shipping and regulations against the opportunity for expanded sales.

While assessing your options, don't overlook niche-specific dropshipping models. Some dropshippers specialise in areas such as eco-friendly products, tech gadgets, or fashion items. A niche-specific model can build your expertise rapidly and create a dedicated customer base, but it may take longer to find a profitable niche and could limit your market reach.

Let's also talk about supplier choices. Will you dropship from domestic suppliers or source products from overseas manufacturers? Domestic suppliers often yield faster shipping times and easier communication; however, they might offer a narrower product selection and higher prices. Overseas suppliers, particularly in manufacturing-heavy countries like China, can provide lower costs and a vast selection, but you'll likely face longer shipping times and potential communication barriers.

Consider the financial aspects of your dropshipping model as well. Some models require more upfront investment but yield higher profit margins, such as stocking products in bulk from a wholesaler and then dropshipping them to your customers. Others need less cash to start but may have tighter margins, like working with a supplier that offers on-demand dropshipping services.

Subscription-based dropshipping is another innovative model where customers sign up for recurring deliveries of products. This offers the advantage of predictable, recurring revenue, but requires you to maintain a consistently high-quality service and product offering to retain customers.

The platform you choose to host your dropshipping store is crucial too. From third-party marketplaces like Amazon or eBay to creating your own e-commerce website on platforms like Shopify or WooCommerce, each option has its pros and cons related to customer reach, fees, customization, and control.

Some entrepreneurs prefer the high-touch dropshipping model, involving personalized products or custom packaging. This can distinguish your brand and command higher prices, however, it necessitates close coordination with your supplier and may limit your scaling capabilities.

In contrast, a low-touch model focuses on simplicity and volume. Here you might sell more generic products with less customization, aiming for a wider audience and streamlined operations. This model usually requires less daily involvement but can also mean more competition and lower profit margins.

Automation is another significant factor. Leveraging automation tools can streamline your dropshipping business, handling everything from pricing adjustments to order processing. However, this comes at the cost of less direct control over daily operations and may lead to additional expenses for the technology utilized.

Risk tolerance is also a personal factor that should influence your choice of dropshipping model. Some models are riskier but offer higher rewards, like focusing on high-ticket items that yield more profit per sale. Conversely, other models focus on lower-cost items with smaller profit margins but also entail less financial risk.

Consider your commitment to environmental and ethical practices. If sustainability and ethical business practices are important to you, you'll need to vet suppliers even more thoroughly and may opt for a dropshipping model that emphasizes these elements, even if it means potentially higher costs or stricter supplier requirements.

Ultimately, your decision-making will benefit from a clear understanding of your target audience. Knowing who your customers are, what they value, and how they shop will guide you towards a dropshipping model that can cater effectively to their needs and preferences.

To sum up, choosing a dropshipping model requires a delicate balance of personal preferences, market understanding, and logistics management. As you ponder these facets, remember that the most successful dropshipping businesses are agile, always prepared to pivot and adapt to a steadily evolving market.

No model is permanently set in stone. Many dropshippers start with one approach and evolve into another as their experience grows and market dynamics change. Your dropshipping journey will be unique, and the model you choose today can evolve as you carve out your corner of the online retail landscape.

Chapter 2:
Setting Up Your Dropshipping Empire

After exploring the ins and outs of dropshipping, it's time to roll up your sleeves and dive into the nuts and bolts of materializing your vision. Establishing a dropshipping business is akin to building a structure: it requires a sturdy foundation, precise blueprints, and the right tools for the job. This chapter will guide you through the essential steps of creating a robust online platform that not only stands out in a crowded marketplace but is also optimized for maximum functionality and user engagement. Before we delve into the intricacies of crafting your online presence or selecting a hosting service that ensures your website remains accessible and responsive, remember that each decision you make at this stage sets the tone for your business's operational efficiency and brand perception. As you embark on this journey, consider that every component, from website design to the usability, works in concert to establish the empire you envision - an empire that's not built overnight but through meticulous planning and strategic execution.

Crafting Your Online Presence

Transitioning from the underpinning mechanics of a dropshipping business, it's crucial to pivot towards the digital storefront you'll present to the world—your online presence. This facet of your business is far more than just a website; it embodies your brand's identity, ethos, and your dialogue with potential customers. Crafting a robust online presence is your ticket to captivating an audience and converting visitors into loyal customers.

Getting started, think of your online presence as the virtual equivalent of a brick-and-mortar store's location, layout, and decor. The Internet is your high street and your website, social media profiles, and every other digital touchpoint come together to form an ecosystem where your brand comes to life. It isn't just about aesthetics either, but also functionality, accessibility, and the overall user experience.

Begin with a clear, concise domain name that resonates with your brand and is easy to remember. Your domain name is the foundation of your brand's online real estate and should be chosen with foresight and consideration. Avoid convoluted or excessively long names that might confuse potential customers or make it hard for them to find you.

Branding goes beyond selecting a catchy name; it incorporates the design elements that will be consistent across all platforms. This includes a memorable logo, a harmonious color palette, and a typeface that aligns with your brand's personality. These elements should reflect the ethos of your products and the expectations of your target audience because they will set the tone for all customer interactions.

Establishing a social media strategy is another imperative layer. Social platforms afford you unprecedented access to targeted audiences where you can engage directly with potential buyers. Present a consistent brand voice and imagery across various networks like Facebook, Instagram, Twitter, and even emerging platforms where your target market might have a presence.

Content is king in the realm of online presence. High-quality, informative content can drive traffic, influence purchasing decisions, and position your brand as an authority in your niche. Deploy a range of content types, from in-depth blog posts and how-to guides to striking product images and engaging videos that tell your brand's story and value proposition.

Email marketing, while traditional, still holds significant sway in nurturing leads and fostering customer loyalty. Gather email subscribers through your website and social media channels, offering them value through newsletters, exclusive discounts, and updates on the latest products and industry news.

Search engine optimization (SEO) is a critical component of your online presence. Optimizing your website and content for search engines is a comprehensive effort that pays dividends in organic search visibility and traffic. Use relevant keywords, meta tags, and structured data to climb the search engine rankings and become more discoverable by potential customers.

Pay attention to the mobile responsiveness of your website. With an increasing number of consumers shopping on their phones, a mobile-friendly site isn't optional—it's essential. The user experience on mobile devices should be just as seamless and satisfying as on a desktop.

Customer reviews and testimonials can significantly influence purchasing choices and enhance credibility. Integrate a system for collecting and displaying reviews to showcase satisfied customers and their experiences with your brand, which can boost confidence for others to follow suit.

While crafting your online presence, you shouldn't overlook the power of analytics. Leveraging tools like Google Analytics provides you with insights into user behavior, traffic sources, conversion rates, and much more. Utilize this data to refine and adapt your online strategy, continually improving the customer experience.

Security is another cornerstone of a reliable online presence. Ensure your site is protected with SSL encryption to secure customer data and transactions. This not only guards against potential cyber threats but also builds trust with your visitors, showing them that their safety is a priority for your brand.

Your online presence should also incorporate clear calls-to-action (CTAs) that guide users through the purchasing process. Whether it's a "Buy Now" button or an invitation to subscribe to your newsletter, compelling CTAs can nudge visitors in the direction you want them to go, helping to boost conversion rates.

The checkout process on your website must be straightforward and hassle-free. Offer multiple payment options, transparent shipping information, and a simple way to resolve issues should they arise. This part of your online presence is critical as it is the point where browsing transforms into buying.

In conclusion, crafting your online presence is a multi-faceted endeavor that requires careful thought and ongoing effort. It's about balancing the visual, the technical, and the strategic elements to create a cohesive, captivating platform that speaks directly to your target audience. It's your digital handshake, the first and lasting impression you make on customers, and your most persuasive salesperson—all rolled into one. Building this presence isn't just about creating an online shop; it's about crafting an empire that stands out in the expansive and ever-changing digital marketplace.

Selecting the Right Hosting Service

After having established a clear vision for your online storefront, the next critical step in launching your dropshipping empire is to choose a hosting service that aligns with your business's needs. This decision isn't one to be taken lightly; your hosting provider is, in essence, the digital foundation of your shop. You'll need a service that not only ensures optimal load times and minimal downtime—who wants to lose sales because a site won't load or is offline?—but also one that scales with your business as it grows. Look for hosting plans that provide robust support, reliable uptime statistics, and seamless integration with your chosen eCommerce platform. Security is also paramount, so prioritize hosts that offer robust protection against cyber threats. While cost-effectiveness is a consideration, remember that your hosting service's performance could make or break your business. Striking a balance between affordability, functionality, and scalability is key in positioning your online store for success.

Building a User-Friendly Website

Building a User-Friendly Website is a crucial step in setting up your dropshipping empire. After solidifying your online presence and selecting a reliable hosting service, the focus must shift towards how your website interacts with its users. It's not just about looks; functionality, simplicity, and intuitiveness are the bedrock of a website that converts visitors into paying customers.

Think of your website as a digital storefront. When customers walk in, they should be met with clear signage, organized shelves, and helpful assistance. Similarly, a user-friendly website must have easy navigation, well-categorized products, and readily available support. Start by brainstorming the architecture of your site, considering how easily information can be accessed and ensuring that it aligns with standard e-commerce practices.

Usability can significantly impact your success, and it begins with speed. A slow-loading site can deter customers faster than you can say "dropshipping." Invest in optimizing your website's load times by compressing images, utilizing caching, and minifying code where possible. Users tend to abandon websites that take longer than a few seconds to load, which is an eternity in the digital world.

Design plays a critical role in usability. A clean, uncluttered layout allows users to focus on what's important—your products. Consistent color schemes and fonts not only strengthen brand identity but also prevent user confusion. Remember, every element on your webpage should serve a purpose, whether it's guiding users towards a purchase or providing essential product information.

While beauty lies in simplicity, functionality should never be compromised. Features like a persistent search bar, filters for products, and an easy-to-use checkout process are non-negotiable in the pursuit of user-friendliness. Mobile responsiveness is another key factor, with a majority of online shoppers using their smartphones to browse and buy. Ensure that your site is fully functional and aesthetically pleasing on all devices.

Trustworthiness is an integral aspect of any user-friendly website. Display customer reviews, return policies, and secure checkout badges prominently. These elements reassure your visitors that they are dealing with a legitimate and customer-focused business. Privacy policy and terms of service should be clearly accessible to build further trust.

Accessibility must also be a priority. Your website should be navigable by everyone, including those with disabilities. Incorporate alternative text for images, ensure that your site is navigable with a keyboard alone, and adhere to other web accessibility guidelines. This is not only a moral imperative but also expands your potential customer base.

Content on your website should be informative and easy to digest. Engaging product descriptions and clear, concise policies aid in decision-making. Remember that your content reflects your brand's voice, so keep it consistent and aligned with your values. Utilize headings and bullet points to break up text for better readability.

Customer support options should be visible and accessible throughout the customer's browsing experience. Live chat features, FAQs, and easy-to-find contact information help answer questions and resolve issues promptly. Providing excellent preemptive support can make or break the user-friendliness of your website.

Regularly testing and updating your website is mandatory to ensure ongoing user-friendliness. Conduct user testing with individuals from your target audience to gain insights into their interaction with your website. Utilize this feedback to make necessary adjustments and stay up-to-date with the latest e-commerce trends and technologies.

Technical reliability goes hand-in-hand with user-friendliness. A website that frequently crashes or contains broken links is a recipe for lost sales. Partner with a quality web hosting service and consider content delivery networks (CDNs) to improve uptime and global performance.

Lastly, always keep the checkout process as simple as possible. A complicated or lengthy checkout can deter potential purchases. Offer multiple payment options, don't force account creation, and clearly state shipping costs and delivery times to prevent any last-minute surprises that might lead to cart abandonment.

In conclusion, building a user-friendly website for your dropshipping business is multifaceted. It requires a keen understanding of web design principles, consideration of the user's experience, and meticulous attention to the operational aspects of your digital storefront. Constant refinement based on user feedback and performance data will keep your website at the forefront of user-friendliness.

By cultivating a user-friendly environment, you lay the foundation for not just attracting customers, but fostering loyalty and repeat business. Having covered the essential elements that contribute to a user-friendly website, you're now poised to create an online experience that resonates with your audience and drives your dropshipping business forward.

Now that you have a grasp on how to build a website optimized for user experience, it's time to delve into finding your unique place in the market. In the next chapter, we'll discuss 'Finding Your Niche in the Market', focusing on how to analyze market trends and identify profitable niches that align with your brand, which is critical for the success of any dropshipping enterprise.

Chapter 3:
Finding Your Niche in the Market

Having laid the crucial groundwork for your online empire, the quest to carve out your distinct space in the bustling market awaits. In this crowded digital bazaar, discovering a niche that is both profitable and resonates with your personal interests isn't just beneficial—it's essential for survival. This quest requires a keen eye for detail and a willingness to dive deeper into consumer needs, ensuring your offerings don't just blend into the background. Astute entrepreneurs know that the sweet spot lies at the intersection of unmet needs and their own passions. They conduct thorough analysis, spot emerging trends, and filter out the ephemeral from the enduring. Such diligence allows them to maneuver through market currents deftly, anchoring their business in a niche that is not only lucrative but also sustainable in the long haul, setting the stage for strategic product selection and successful brand positioning in upcoming chapters.

Analyzing Market Trends

Embarking on the journey to find your niche within the vast landscape of online markets requires more than a keen sense of business; it involves a methodical analysis of market trends. Understanding these trends can lay the groundwork for pinpointing a profitable niche that resonates with consumers, placing you at a significant advantage over competition.

First and foremost, it's vital to grasp the concept of a market trend. In essence, market trends are the movements and directions that markets take over a period of time. These trends can be dictated by a multitude of factors, including technological advancements, cultural shifts, economic changes, and consumer behavior patterns. By keeping an eye on these elements, you can forecast the potential demand for products or services within your dropshipping business.

Data analysis tools have become indispensable in today's digital marketplace. They offer insight into consumer habits and preferences by tracking online behavior, sales data, and search engine usage. To make the most of these tools, look into software that provides real-time analytics on marketplaces such as Amazon, eBay, or other ecommerce platforms where dropshipping is prevalent.

Part of analyzing market trends involves observing the competition. You'll want to take note of what products are being offered, pricing strategies, marketing tactics, and the customer experience they're providing. Competitor analysis can serve as a beacon, guiding you to gaps in the market that you can fill with your unique value proposition.

Understanding your target demographic is another crucial element. Market trends can differ vastly depending on the age, gender, location, and interests of your intended audience. Platforms like Google Analytics present a wealth of demographic data, allowing dropshippers to tailor their approach to align more closely with who their customers are and what they seek.

Staying current with the latest trends might also entail attending industry trade shows, subscribing to relevant magazines, and participating in online forums. Such activities can provide you with the earliest insights into up-and-coming products and consumer trends, often before they hit the mainstream.

Social media platforms are real-time indicators of consumer interests and market trends. By monitoring hashtags, influencer posts, and social media advertisements, you can gather invaluable information about product popularity and market dynamics. This type of qualitative data is essential for making informed decisions in your dropshipping endeavors.

Seasonal trends should not be underestimated. Products often rise and fall in demand based on seasons and holidays. This cyclical knowledge can help you anticipate shifts in the market, allowing you to stock up or diversify your offerings to capitalize on these timely events.

Economic indicators such as consumer spending reports and gross domestic product (GDP) growth can also provide insights into the overall health of the market. These broad indicators can help you assess consumer confidence and predict buying behaviors that may directly impact your dropshipping business.

Feedback and communication with existing customers are invaluable for recognizing market trends. Encourage reviews, conduct surveys, and engage with your audience to gain a deeper understanding of their ongoing needs and desires. This direct feedback loop can lead to adjustments in your product offerings that are more in tune with the marketplace.

Technological trends also have a monumental impact on product demand. The rise of smart home devices, health-tech wearables, and eco-friendly products are just a few examples of how tech trends have created niches that dropshippers can profit from. Stay informed about tech breakthroughs and how they might influence consumer choices and opportunities for your business.

Cultural movements, such as sustainability and mindfulness, have given way to new market niches. Embracing and understanding the values behind these movements can position you to cater to audiences looking for products that reflect their ethical and philosophical ideals.

Subscription services and the demand for unique, personalized experiences represent another trend of note. This encourages dropshippers to think beyond one-time sales and consider how to create recurring revenue through subscription-based models or by offering customizable products.

Lastly, forecast reports published by market research firms can offer a more official and comprehensive perspective on potential trends. These reports, while sometimes costly, can be a worthwhile investment, providing in-depth analyses based on extensive consumer data that can be leveraged for your dropshipping business's future strategies.

To sum up, analyzing market trends is an ongoing process that requires attention to detail, an open mind, and the willingness to adapt. Your ability to anticipate and react to these market shifts is paramount in carving out a sustainable niche and ensuring the long-term success of your dropshipping business. By staying attuned to the ebb and flow of market trends and employing a mix of quantitative and qualitative research tactics, you'll set the foundation for a thriving online venture.

Identifying Profitable Niches

As we transition from grasping the overarching market trends, it's now critical to zoom in on the lifeblood of any successful dropshipping business — finding a profitable niche. Identifying such niches requires a blend of strategic thinking, market research, and consumer behavior understanding. It's about pinpointing a section of the market that is both underserved and ready for growth.

First and foremost, a profitable niche should reflect an area of the market where customer demand is not being fully met by current offerings. This means deploying data-fueled tools to discover keyword searches that abound with potential yet suffer from a lack of sufficient suppliers. In other words, you're looking for a gap in the market where there are more potential customers than there are products available.

One important aspect of this discovery process is analyzing marketplaces like Amazon, eBay, and Etsy. By deep-diving into bestseller lists, new and trending products, or even sections labeled "customers also bought," one can unearth hidden gems. This method provides valuable insights into consumer preferences and emerging trends that aren't yet saturated by competition.

The next step involves examining search engine data using tools like Google Trends or SEMrush. You want to spot patterns that suggest recurring interest or a burgeoning rise in certain product categories. Be alert for keywords that show a high volume of searches but low competition, indicating a niche ripe for entry.

Social media platforms are also treasure troves of data that can help identify profitable niches. Through listening to consumer conversations and gauging their reactions to certain products or brands, you can anticipate which market segments are on the cusp of popularity. Monitoring hashtags, influencers, and community groups could unveil niches that the market has overlooked.

Additionally, you must consider the financial viability of potential niches. Some products may be popular but offer slim profit margins due to high shipping costs or low price points dictated by the market. Therefore, your analysis must go beyond popularity and include potential profitability, considering aspects such as product size, weight, and average selling price.

Customer pain points are another goldmine for identifying profitable niches. Engage in forums, read reviews, and conduct surveys to grasp what frustrates consumers about existing products. Often, addressing a specific pain point can catapult a niche product to success because you deliver a targeted solution to a well-defined problem.

Do not disregard the importance of passion and expertise. While these should not completely drive your niche selection, they play a vital role in sustaining your interest and providing authentic, knowledgeable service to your customers. Seamlessly blending passion and a profitable niche can make for a powerful combination.

Once a potential niche is identified, validate your idea by testing the waters. This might involve setting up a landing page to measure interest or using pay-per-click advertising to gauge consumer reactions. Pre-launch strategies can be instrumental in confirming or refuting your niche hypothesis before fully committing to product sourcing and website development.

Remember, not all niches are created equal. Trends may tempt you, but sustainability should be the cornerstone of your decision. Short-lived trends can offer quick wins, but niches rooted in steady, long-term demand provide a foundation for lasting success. Aim to strike a balance between trending and timeless products to ensure both immediate and enduring relevance.

Competitor analysis is crucial in identifying your place in the niche landscape. Look at direct and indirect competitors to understand their strengths and weaknesses and discover opportunities for differentiation. You might find a sub-niche where you can excel or a unique angle on a popular product that sets you apart.

Consider the economic health and trajectory of your potential niche. Conducting market research that factors in economic indicators like consumer spending habits and disposable income variations can prevent a venture into a niche that is liable to shrink or vanish due to economic downturns.

Lastly, keep an eye on regulatory changes or potential legal constraints. For instance, niches involving health supplements or tech products may have strict guidelines that can influence your ability to market them effectively. Meticulous research here can save you from investing in a niche with potential legal challenges.

As the canvas of market niches is broad and ever-evolving, staying flexible and informed is non-negotiable. The niche that looks promising today may be entirely different tomorrow, so a profitable niche is not just about identifying; it's about adapting and evolving alongside the market.

In summary, identifying a profitable niche is a critical step that requires diligence, creativity, and a bit of daring. Through methodical research and strategic analysis, you can uncover niches that are perfectly poised for profitability. Cultivate the ability to spot opportunities where others haven't, and you might just find yourself at the forefront of a lucrative online dropshipping enterprise.

Chapter 4:
Sourcing Products and Suppliers

With a firm grasp on market trends and a clear niche identified, we now pivot to the crucial task of sourcing products and suppliers. This chapter dives into the essential strategies for discovering reputable dropshipping companies capable of providing not only a vast selection of products but also reliability and quality support. It's about striking the right balance; you'll need to ensure that the products you select resonate with your target audience yet remain feasible and profitable to offer. We'll focus on tactics for building strong relationships with these vital partners in your dropshipping journey while navigating the complexities of managing supply chains. Product sourcing isn't just an operational necessity—it's a strategic move that will dictate the success and scalability of your online business.

Where to Look for Reputable Dropshipping Companies

Having navigated the fundamentals of dropshipping and identified your niche, the natural progression is to find the companies that will serve as the backbone of your product fulfillment. Locating reputable dropshipping companies is crucial to the success of your business. A reliable supplier ensures product quality, timely shipping, and responsive service. But where do you begin your search for these cornerstone partners?

The internet is vast with databases and directories dedicated to dropshipping suppliers. One of the first stops on your supplier discovery journey should be online dropshipping directories. These platforms list numerous suppliers and provide valuable insights such as reviews, product ranges, and quality indicators. Some popular directories include SaleHoo, Worldwide Brands, and Doba. They work to curate a list of vetted suppliers, saving you time and reducing the risk of encountering fraudulent operations.

Another online treasure trove for dropshippers is industry-specific trade shows and virtual events. These can be invaluable resources for connecting with suppliers and manufacturers directly. By attending these events, you can network with professionals, gain industry insights, witness product demonstrations, and forge meaningful business relationships.

Trade publications and online forums are not to be underestimated; they often provide recommendations for trusted suppliers within specific industries. By actively participating in and monitoring discussions in these spaces, you can learn from other entrepreneurs' experiences and find suppliers that have been verified by your peers.

Manufacturer sourcing is an underrated route; it involves contacting the product manufacturers directly. If they're willing to dropship, you can bypass middlemen. Alternatively, they might refer you to distributors who handle their dropshipping, thus ensuring legitimacy and product authenticity.

There's also value in leveraging the power of search engines with regular online research. A careful scrutiny of suppliers' online presence, customer feedback, and reputation can unearth some solid options. Be sure to utilize advanced search techniques to find suppliers who may not be as prominently advertised but offer competitive services.

Social media platforms present yet another avenue. Many suppliers use these channels to engage with customers, showcase their products, and market their brands. By searching for dropshipping suppliers on platforms like Facebook, Instagram, and LinkedIn, you can gauge their market presence and customer interaction quality.

B2B Wholesale marketplaces such as Alibaba, AliExpress, and others have also become hotspots for finding dropshipping suppliers. While they require due diligence to ensure supplier credibility, these platforms allow you to source globally and have a vast variety of products to choose from.

Competitor analysis should not be overlooked. By investigating where your competitors are sourcing their products, you can discover experienced dropshipping suppliers who are already familiar with the online retail process. This can be done by reverse-searching product images or looking up product codes and seeing which suppliers are providing them.

When considering an online marketplace, always keep an eye on their customer support and service standards. A supplier with a strong support system is more likely to handle customer inquiries and issues effectively, reflecting well on your business. Reach out to them with inquiries and evaluate their responsiveness and helpfulness as part of your vetting process.

Local trade groups and chambers of commerce can also serve as valuable resources for finding suppliers. They typically have connections with a wide variety of businesses, including those that may offer dropshipping services. Participation in local business events can open doors to partnerships that might not be advertised online.

Be brave enough to explore industry publications, both physical and digital. This old-school method still holds merit because suppliers often advertise their services or may be featured in articles or case studies within these publications. Scouring through them can lead to fruitful connections with established suppliers.

Lastly, caution should accompany any search. While there are many reputable dropshipping companies out there, scams and low-quality suppliers are equally prevalent. It's essential to perform thorough due diligence by checking for business licenses, requesting product samples, reading testimonials, and ensuring clear and coherent communication before forging a partnership.

In finding suppliers, patience and resilience are virtues. It might not be an overnight success, but forming the right connections will set a solid foundation for your dropshipping business. Cross-reference potential suppliers against multiple sources, use every tool at your disposal, and never settle for less than your business deserves.

The subsequent section, 'Building Relationships with Suppliers,' will delve into creating and nurturing a solid and mutually beneficial relationship with the suppliers you've chosen. For now, focus on the search, and don't rush this critical step – your future self and business will thank you for the diligence and attention to detail.

Building Relationships with Suppliers

Maintaining strong relationships with suppliers is crucial for ensuring your dropshipping business thrives. Initially, approach each interaction with transparency to lay the groundwork for mutual trust. Recognize that timely communication, reliability in following through on agreements, and understanding the supplier's needs and constraints are key to building a robust partnership. Don't hesitate to ask questions about their production capacities, lead times, and quality control processes—it's essential to be on the same page. It's equally important to negotiate terms that benefit both parties; this might include discussing bulk order discounts or faster shipping options to improve your offering. As your business grows, these relationships can evolve into exclusive deals or collaborations that secure your market position and provide stability in your supply chain. While contracts are crucial, remember that a personable approach, showing appreciation for their service, and regular check-ins can go a long way in keeping the relationship positive and responsive, which in the fast-paced online marketplace can give you a critical edge.

Developing a Winning Product Selection Strategy begins with a systematic approach that merges market research, supplier analysis, and a keen understanding of consumer behavior. The right product selection can mean the difference between a thriving online business and one that struggles to make sales. Let's delve into the crucial steps and considerations that form the backbone of an effective product selection strategy for your dropshipping business.

Understand Your Market and Audience

First and foremost, you must have a clear understanding of your target market. What are their needs, preferences, and shopping behaviors? Use tools such as Google Trends and social media analytics to gather data on what products your target audience is discussing, searching for, and purchasing. Knowing your audience helps in aligning your product selection with their expectations, potentially increasing the likelihood of conversions.

Assess Product Viability

Every item you consider should go through a viability filter. This includes an evaluation of the product's potential profitability, shipping considerations, demand consistency, and how well it aligns with your brand. Tools like Google Keyword Planner can provide insight into the search volume for products, indicating demand levels.

Additionally, check for potential legal restrictions or complications associated with selling certain products.

Analyze Competition

While it's essential to find products that are in demand, it's equally important to assess the level of competition. If a market is oversaturated, it could drive up advertising costs and make it harder to secure a sale. Investigate the market to identify gaps that you can capitalize on, or find ways to offer a unique value proposition for products that are in high competition.

Work with Reliable Suppliers

The suppliers you choose will be pivotal to your dropshipping success. They must have a reputation for product quality, reliability, and responsive communication. Use directories and wholesale platforms to find potential suppliers and meticulously review their terms, conditions, and reviews before forming a business relationship. Remember, your supplier's weaknesses can quickly become your own.

Consider Profit Margins

Pricing is critical in dropshipping. You'll need to select products with enough room in their cost structure to mark up for profit, without pricing yourself out of the market. Be diligent in calculating all costs—including goods, shipping, taxes, and platform fees—when evaluating potential products for your store. Additionally, consider the perceived value of products, as customers are often willing to pay more for items they deem premium or unique.

Product Quality and Compliance

Low-quality products lead to unhappy customers and, ultimately, harm your brand's reputation. Make sure to request samples and inspect product quality firsthand. In addition, ensure that your products comply with standards and regulations relevant to your target markets. Neglecting this step can result in legal problems and customer safety issues.

Opt for Evergreen or Trending Products

Some products maintain steady demand over time (evergreen), while others may experience sudden spikes in popularity due to seasonal trends or viral moments (trending). Combining a mix of both evergreen and trending products can balance the stability and excitement in your inventory, each serving their purpose to attract and retain customers.

Use Data-Driven Decision-Making

Opinions and gut feelings are helpful, but data should drive your product selection process. Utilize analytics, market reports, and sales data to make informed choices about which products to include in your dropshipping store. This may involve tracking metrics over time to identify trends, best-sellers, and underperformers.

Factor in Shipping and Handling

Products that are large, heavy, fragile, or have special shipping requirements can complicate the dropshipping process. Opt for items that are easy to ship and handle to reduce potential headaches with logistics and customer satisfaction. This doesn't mean avoiding larger items altogether, but these factors should be carefully considered.

Carry Out Testing and Validation

Before committing to a wide range of products, test the market. This could involve the use of A/B testing on small-scale ad campaigns to see which products receive a stronger reaction or sales performance. It reduces risk and can save you from investing too heavily in inventory that might not sell well.

Watch for Seasonal Shifts and Trends

Consumer behavior changes with the seasons and with emerging trends. Make sure to adjust your product offerings to align with current events, holidays, and seasons to maximize your chances of capturing relevant traffic and sales.

Listen to Customer Feedback

Your customers are a valuable source of information. Listen to their feedback about your products, both what they love and what they believe could improve. Use this feedback to fine-tune your product offerings. Positive reviews can validate your current selection, while constructive criticism can guide your future strategies.

Stay Flexible and Adaptable

The online marketplace is ever-changing. Stay adaptable in your approach to product selection. Be ready to phase out items that aren't performing and introduce new ones in response to evolving consumer interests and market dynamics.

By focusing on these key elements, your dropshipping business will stand far better odds at curating a selection of products that resonates with your target audience, remains competitive in the marketplace, and drives sustainable success. Remember, a winning product selection strategy is an ongoing process that will develop and improve as you gather more data and insights from your dropshipping journey.

Chapter 5:
Maximizing Profits Through Pricing

Having navigated the strategic sourcing of products and suppliers, the time has come to dive into one of the most critical aspects of your dropshipping business—pricing. While it may seem straightforward, setting the right price for your products is a delicate balancing act that can significantly impact your bottom line. This chapter sets out to arm you with pricing strategies that boost profitability without alienating your customers. You'll learn how to analyze your costs, understand the perceived value of your offerings, and benchmark against competitors to find that sweet spot. It's important to price competitively, but you also need to ensure that your margins can sustain and grow your business. We'll explore tactics on how to structure your pricing in a way that both entices customers and keeps you in the green. We'll also touch on the psychology of pricing and how small tweaks can make a big difference in sales. Remember, the goal here isn't to undercut the competition at every turn; rather, it's about optimizing your price points so that customers feel they're getting great value while you maximize profits.

Pricing Strategies That Work

As we delve into the tactics of maximizing profits, it's crucial to craft pricing strategies that do more than merely exist; they need to work effectively in fostering your online dropshipping business. Establishing the right price points can mean the difference between thriving and merely surviving in the competitive digital marketplace.

Firstly, it's essential to understand the psychology of pricing. Setting a price that's too low might lead to high sales volumes yet slim profit margins, while pricing too high may deter potential customers. Striking a balance is key, and often, prices that end on a .99 or .97 are perceived as better deals, even though the difference is minuscule.

Demand-based pricing is a dynamic approach that can be particularly potent. By monitoring the demand for your products and adjusting prices accordingly, you can capitalize on trends and maximize profits. However, be cautious not to fluctuate prices too wildly, as that can frustrate customers.

Competitive pricing is another strategy to consider. You need to be aware of what rivals are charging for similar items and ensure your prices are in line—or cleverly, a touch lower. But do remember, competing solely on price can be perilous, encouraging a race to the bottom that can erode your brand's perceived value. Aim to complement low prices with other value propositions.

Value-based pricing, where you set prices primarily on the perceived value to the customer, can help differentiate your products. By highlighting unique benefits or superior quality, you can justify a higher price point and attract discerning buyers who are less price-sensitive.

Bundling products is a strategy not to be overlooked in the realm of pricing. By offering complementary items as a package at a slightly reduced rate, you can increase perceived value, move more products, and uplift profits through higher average order values.

Consider implementing tiered pricing, which can entice customers to purchase more by offering lower unit prices at higher quantities.

This approach is beneficial as it not only increases sales volume but also improves inventory turnover.

Penetration pricing can give a new product the boost it needs to seize market share. Setting an introductory low price can lure in customers, but this strategy requires a careful eventual increase in price to ensure profitability over time.

Adopting psychological pricing is about aligning with the way consumers think. Price points that convey affordability or luxury can trigger the desired emotional response, whether that means setting a price just below a round number or pricing in alignment with high-end expectations.

Skimming is the practice of starting with a high price and lowering it over time. This tactic works best for innovative products or those first-to-market, letting you initially target early adopters willing to pay a premium before addressing the broader market.

Loss-leader pricing can be particularly effective in the online retail landscape. It involves selling a product at a loss to draw customers in, with the expectation that once they've arrived, they'll make additional purchases at profitable margins.

Lastly, don't forget the importance of regular price evaluations. The ebb and flow of the online market mean what works today may not work tomorrow. Assess your strategies, test different price points, and adjust based on results and customer feedback to keep your pricing strategy sharp and successful.

By employing a mix of these pricing strategies, you can build a robust framework that not only supports your business's profitability but also resonates well with your customer base. Pricing should be a thoughtful ingredient in your business recipe, one that's revisited and refined as your business grows and market conditions evolve.

It's also worth mentioning that transparency in pricing can bolster customer trust. Hidden fees or unexpected charges at checkout can lead customers to abandon their carts. Clear, upfront pricing without nasty surprises can enhance the customer experience and encourage repeat business.

In crafting these strategies, incorporate A/B testing, where you present two price points to different cohorts and analyze which generates superior outcomes. Employing such data-driven techniques can help you refine your pricing approach with precision.

With these pricing strategies in place, you are better positioned to turn your dropshipping endeavors into a profitable venture. The key is to remain nimble, attuned to both your customers and competitors, and to continuously optimize your pricing tactics for maximum effect.

Competing on Price Without Sacrificing Margins

Understanding how to compete on price, while keeping your margins healthy, is essential for the longevity of your online dropshipping business. The key to successful pricing is not simply to undercut competitors, but to offer value to your customers in a way that maintains profitability. In this section, we will discuss strategies and insights that can allow you to remain competitive without compromising your margins.

Begin by examining your cost structure in detail. Know exactly what your expenses are, including the cost of goods, shipping, packaging, transaction fees, and advertising. Effective cost control is the foundation that allows you flexibility in pricing without squeezing your margins too thin.

Look for efficiencies in your supply chain. Can you negotiate better rates with your suppliers based on volume or early payment? Can you reduce packaging costs without compromising product safety or customer unboxing experience? Small cost savings can allow you to reduce prices without affecting your margin.

Differentiate your offerings. Add value through bundling products, creating unique product descriptions, or offering superior customer service. When customers recognize extra value, they are less sensitive to price and more to the overall value they receive.

Leverage loss leaders strategically. Identify products that you can afford to sell at a low margin or even at cost as a way to draw customers into your store. Make sure these products are complemented by other items in your store that can be sold at a higher margin. The goal is to increase overall basket size and margin.

Use psychological pricing techniques. Prices that end in '9' or '.99' are perceived as better deals than rounded numbers. Use this strategy to create an impression of value even when your prices are not the absolute lowest on the market.

Implement dynamic pricing models where feasible. Monitor your competition and market demand to adjust prices in a way that you stay competitive but not at the expense of your profits. Prices can be flexible - low during off-peak times and higher when demand spikes.

Focus on building a strong brand. Customers are willing to pay more for products from a brand they trust. Invest in building a positive reputation which can give you more flexibility to price above competitors without risking sales.

Consider the long-term lifetime value of a customer over the transactional value. It may be worthwhile to reduce margins temporarily to acquire a customer, particularly if your data shows they are likely to make repeat purchases at full margin in the future.

Time promotions and sales carefully. Instead of across-the-board price cuts, use targeted promotions that create urgency while protecting margins. For example, limited-time offers or clearance sales of end-of-line stock are effective ways to stimulate buying without a blanket reduction in prices.

Engage in value perception marketing. Highlight the features and benefits of your products that justify their price. Explain the quality, the convenience, the after-sale support, or the ethical considerations behind them, whatever sets you apart and creates additional perceived value.

Offer tiered pricing to cater to different market segments. Some customers are willing to pay more for premium options. By segmenting your products or services, you can satisfy bargain hunters and those looking for premium options, maximizing profits across different customer groups.

Utilize membership or loyalty programs to provide value to your customers without lowering prices. Exclusive deals, advance access to sales, or points for purchases can incentivize customers to choose you over a competitor without lowering your prices.

Finally, keep a close eye on your key performance indicators (KPIs). Regularly review your gross profit margin, conversion rates, average order value, and customer acquisition cost. These metrics will tell you if your pricing strategy is working or if you need to make adjustments.

Remember, in the competitive world of dropshipping, you need to stay agile. Test and tweak continuously, while keeping your overarching strategy focused on providing value in a way that customers are willing to pay for. Aiming for the right balance between competitive pricing and healthy margins is crucial, and it's a challenge that can be met with creativity and a focus on efficiency.

By leveraging these strategies, you can carve out a competitive position in the crowded online marketplace. It's about smart pricing, not just low pricing. Strengthen your mindset around value creation and your business won't only survive, but thrive, even in the fiercely competitive dropshipping arena.

Chapter 6:
Crafting the Perfect Sales Funnel

After fine-tuning your pricing strategy, it's time to shift our focus towards the customer's journey through your online store—a journey that defines whether they leave as a buyer or a browser. A well-crafted sales funnel is pivotal for converting visitors into customers and maximizing the value of each purchase. In this chapter, we'll dissect the intricacies of the sales funnel, learning how to align it seamlessly with the thought processes and decision-making patterns of your potential customers. We'll start by unraveling the stages of the customer journey, from awareness to action, and how each step can be optimized to ensure a smooth transition. Next, we jump into creating high-converting landing pages that serve as the entry point of your funnel, compelling visitors to move forward and explore your product offerings. You'll learn how to capture interest, address hesitations, and provide clear paths to purchase through an intuitive design and persuasive copy. What's more, we'll delve into strategies for upsells and cross-sells that not only enhance customer value but also improve their shopping experience by offering complementary products that cater to their needs. Let's embark on this vital part of your dropshipping venture, where you'll discover how to construct a funnel that resonates with your audience, guiding them towards making a purchase, and turning passive interest into active sales.

Understanding the Customer Journey

In the dynamic world of online dropshipping, understanding the customer journey is akin to reading a map before embarking on a treasure hunt. This path from discovery to purchase, replete with varying touchpoints, determines how effectively your sales funnel converts prospects into paying customers.

At its core, the customer journey encompasses the entire spectrum of a consumer's experience with your brand, from the moment they first become aware of your product to the final decision to buy. Each of these steps presents an opportunity to engage with the customer and guide them closer to making a purchase.

Awareness is the inception point of the journey. Potential buyers might encounter your brand through various channels - a sponsored post on social media, a recommendation from a friend, or perhaps a search engine result. Your task is to ensure your presence is strong and positive at these early junctures, making the first impression a compelling invitation to explore further.

As customers move from awareness to consideration, they begin to evaluate your products against their needs and alternatives offered by competitors. Here, detailed product information, customer reviews, and comparisons can play a pivotal role in their decision-making process. It's essential to anticipate and answer the questions that may arise in their minds at this stage.

The conversion step is critical - it is where interest is transformed into action. A streamlined checkout process, clear call-to-action elements, and reassurances of security can significantly reduce cart abandonment rates. Often, this is where your intuitive site design and persuasive product descriptions earn their keep.

Retention follows conversion, though in reality, it's a parallel process that enhances the entire journey. Satisfied customers are more willing to make repeat purchases and become brand advocates. Implementing loyalty programs, offering exclusive deals, and maintaining communication through newsletters are all strategies that can increase customer lifetime value.

For a layer of context, consider the Experience Stage, where customers interact with your product after purchase. The quality of your product, the efficiency of shipping, and the effectiveness of your customer service can turn a one-time buyer into a loyal customer. Address their concerns promptly, and they may spread word-of-your brand.

Advocacy comes when happy customers recommend your products to others, effectively kickstarting a new customer journey. This organic marketing cannot be underestimated, as word-of-mouth is impactful in building trust with new prospects.

It's important to remember that not all customer journeys are linear. Digital points of sale allow for a more chaotic journey, where customers might hop between stages before making a final decision. Hence, your sales funnel should cater to a non-linear path, offering several entry and exit points.

Data collection and analysis are crucial in understanding how customers are interacting with your brand at each stage. Tools like Google Analytics and customer relationship management (CRM) systems can trace a customer's path and reveal patterns and trends that can inform your strategies.

Personalization elevates the customer journey, making the potential buyer feel understood and valued. Use the data at your disposal to tailor the shopping experience to individual preferences. By showing related items or remembering past searches, you can create a more engaging and seamless experience.

During the decision-making process, the role of value cannot be overstated. Customers consider what they gain versus what they expend. This isn't limited to monetary cost - it encompasses time, effort, and emotional investment as well. Your funnel should streamline the perceived exertion at every turn, highlighting the benefits clearly and concisely.

Technology has birthed multiple channels for customers to engage with. From mobile apps to social media platforms, ensure that each touchpoint is optimized for engagement. Consistency across these channels builds a cohesive brand experience, removing friction and encouraging progress towards purchase.

Overcoming objections is an integral part of the journey. Frequently, customers encounter internal or external hesitations. By providing guarantees, return policies, and exemplary pre-sale support, you can help assuade doubts and move the customer towards a confident purchase decision.

In concluding this chapter, grasp the fact that crafting the perfect sales funnel necessitates a thorough understanding of the customer journey. It's about creating a clear, inviting path that leads from curiosity to satisfaction. Analyzing each stage, optimizing interactions, and fostering relationships will strengthen your dropshipping business and keep customers returning for more.

With the customer journey mapped out, the next natural progression is to build the channels that'll host this journey - creating high-converting landing pages. That transformational piece of digital real estate is where your funnel strategy becomes tangible and your understanding of the customer journey begins to reap rewards.

Creating High-Converting Landing Pages

Landing pages act as the digital welcome mat to your online dropshipping business, urging potential customers to take the plunge and explore your offerings. In crafting these crucial pages, clarity and purpose must coalesce to secure a visitor's commitment without a moment's hesitation. Featuring bold headlines that resonate with your target audience, coupled with an intuitive design, a well-constructed landing page presents a clear value proposition and utilizes persuasive call-to-action (CTA) buttons to usher users through the desired action funnel. Visually compelling imagery and testimonials add credibility, while tight copy enhances the messaging without crowding the user's journey. Offering an exclusive deal or incentive can be the tipping point for conversion, but there's also magic in the details—ensuring fast load times, mobile responsiveness, and seamless navigation is essential. Continual testing and refinement using A/B tests yields invaluable insights, tailoring your landing pages to become an indispensable cog in the seamless operation of your sales funnel, ultimately paving the way for higher conversion rates and increased profit margins.

Utilizing Upsells and Cross-sells

In the vast world of dropshipping, simply making a sale isn't the end of your revenue-generating journey. The art of mastering upsells and cross-sells can significantly boost your bottom line without needing to constantly attract new customers. This strategy requires careful planning and execution but, when done right, it can increase the average order value while enhancing customer satisfaction.

Upselling is the practice of encouraging customers to purchase a higher-end product than the one they are currently considering. For your online dropshipping business, this can mean suggesting a more feature-rich version of a product or a premium model that offers additional benefits. To successfully implement this tactic, you need to understand your customers' needs and present the upsell as a way to better meet those needs.

On the other hand, cross-selling involves recommending related products or accessories that complement the original item being purchased. These suggestions can be made at various stages of the purchase process but are often most effective at the point of sale. When curating cross-sell items, ensure they add value and are contextually relevant to the customer's interests.

One of the key strategies in upselling is timing. Introducing your upsell at the right moment can make all the difference. Typically, the checkout process is an ideal time to suggest additional items as customers are already in a buying mindset. However, ensure that your upsells don't disrupt or complicate the checkout process. A smooth and non-intrusive upsell that feels like a natural part of the transaction is more likely to succeed.

Creating bundles is a great way to incorporate both upsells and cross-sells into your offerings. You can pair complementary products at a slightly lower price than if purchased separately. This not only adds value for the customer but also increases your sales without requiring additional customer acquisition efforts. Plus, bundles simplify decision-making for the customer, making it an effective selling technique.

Another effective approach is to provide a clear comparison between the products being offered and the upsell options. Highlighting the benefits and value of an upgrade or additional item can help customers make an informed decision. Detailed product descriptions and comparison charts that emphasize the advantages of higher-tier products can entice customers to spend more.

Personalization is integral to successful upselling and cross-selling. By using data from customers' previous purchases and browsing history, you can make targeted recommendations that resonate with their specific preferences. Tools like machine learning algorithms and cookies can help in collecting this data and delivering personalized suggestions.

Be mindful of the perceived value of the upsells and cross-sells. Customers are more likely to go for an offer if they perceive it as a good deal. This could involve limited-time offers, exclusive packages, or special discounts for additional purchases made. A sense of scarcity or exclusivity can be a powerful motivator for customers to take advantage of an upsell or cross-sell.

Cross-selling is not just for products; consider offering complementary services as well. If you're selling electronics, offer an extended warranty service as an add-on. For fashion items, suggest style guides or personal shopper services. Services provide an opportunity for recurring revenue that can continue to benefit your business long after the initial sale.

Always aim for a soft sell approach when it comes to upselling and cross-selling. You don't want to come off as pushy or solely interested in making more money. Instead, frame your offers as ways to enhance the customer's experience or to provide solutions that the customer didn't realize they needed.

Test and measure the impact of your upsells and cross-sells. A/B split testing different upsell and cross-sell offers can provide valuable insights into what resonates best with your customers. Look at metrics such as conversion rate, average order value, and customer lifetime value to determine the effectiveness of your cross-selling and upselling strategies.

Remember to follow up post-purchase with customers who opted for an upsell or cross-sell. Customer feedback can be invaluable in refining your approach. A satisfied customer who feels they made the right choice can also become an advocate for your store, potentially drawing in more customers through word-of-mouth.

Traversing the world of upselling and cross-selling is about striking the right balance between increasing sales and maintaining customer trust and satisfaction. By using these strategies judiciously, you're not only maximizing profits but also building deeper relationships with your customers. This practice becomes an integral part of customer experience management in your dropshipping business.

In conclusion, upselling and cross-selling are pivotal techniques for enhancing the profitability of a dropshipping operation. They allow you to maximize each transaction and increase the value you deliver to your customers. With a customer-centric approach and a keen eye on analytics and feedback, you can finesse these strategies to work wonders for your online storefront.

The next layer in the cake of your online business mastery involves branding. As we shift gears toward developing a robust brand identity, remember that the tactics explored in optimizing upsells and cross-sells form the undercurrent that elevates a mere transaction into a holistic, branded shopping experience.

Chapter 7:
The Power of Branding

In the competitive world of online dropshipping, your brand is the distinctive signature that sets you apart from the myriad of others vying for consumer attention. As we delve into the essence of what builds a formidable brand presence, we discover that it's more than just a memorable logo or a catchy tagline; it's the embodiment of your business's personality, values, and promise to your customers. A compelling brand narrative forges a deeper connection with your audience, fostering loyalty and encouraging word-of-mouth marketing. It's not merely about aesthetics; it's about crafting a holistic experience that resonates with your target demographic. By articulating a vision that reflects the aspirations of your customers, you don't just sell products; you offer a lifestyle and an experience that consumers are eager to embrace. In this digital age where authenticity reigns, a well-defined brand can be the beacon that guides customers to your virtual doorstep, transforming first-time buyers into lifelong patrons. Let's unpack the strategic elements that give your brand its power and learn how to harness it to elevate your online dropshipping business.

Developing a Memorable Brand Identity

After exploring the essentials of setting up your online dropshipping business, the next critical step is to establish a unique and memorable brand identity. This goes beyond just a logo or a catchy name; it captures the essence of your business, its values, and the message you want to convey to your potential customers. It's also what sets you apart from the myriad of competitors in the online marketplace.

Your brand identity serves as the cornerstone of all your marketing efforts and customer interactions. It's not merely an outward expression; it radiates from the core of your business strategy. A memorable brand resonates with customers, establishes a loyal customer base, and can even command a premium for your products.

To start this exciting journey, you need to conceptualize your brand. Think of it as creating a personality for your business. Who would your brand be if it were a person? This analogy helps to weave together elements such as tone, style, and ethos into a coherent personality that customers can relate to and remember

Understanding your target audience is another fundamental aspect. Who are they? What do they value? And, most importantly, how does your brand connect with these values? Your brand should speak to your audience's desires and needs, providing a solution that feels tailored just for them.

Visual identity is certainly a vital component — the colors, typography, and imagery that you choose will become synonymous with your brand. These elements should be consistent across all platforms, from your website to your social media profiles, and even your packaging.

A distinct and appealing logo is the centrepiece of your visual identity. It's the most identifiable aspect of your brand for customers. Therefore, it's worth investing time and, if necessary, professional help to get it right. Your logo should communicate what your business is about at a glance and be simple enough to be remembered.

But, it's not all about looks. The voice of your brand is just as significant. How does your brand 'speak' in written communication? Whether it's professional, friendly, quirky, or serious, the tone should be distinctive and consistent in all forms of communication, including advertising copy, social media posts, and customer service interactions.

Storytelling is a powerful tool to enhance your brand identity. It allows you to build a narrative around your brand that helps customers connect on an emotional level. Your brand's story should be authentic and highlight what makes your business unique, especially your journey, challenges, and successes in the dropshipping space.

A solid brand identity should elicit emotions and create experiences. This can be done through thoughtfully crafted packaging, personalized thank you notes, or unexpected bonus features with a purchase. Small gestures can leave a lasting impression and make your brand unforgettable.

It's essential that you deliver on the promises your brand identity makes. Consistency in quality, customer service, and the overall shopping experience safeguard your brand's reputation and encourage customers to return and recommend your business to others.

In a digital world, where customers often interact with brands through screens, having a human element can be a game-changer. Don't shy away from showing the faces behind the brand. Be it through 'behind-the-scenes' content, team introductions, or personal stories, humanizing your brand can go a long way in building trust.

Also integral to your brand identity is a set of core values that define your business ethics and practices. Today's consumers are increasingly concerned about sustainability, transparency, and corporate responsibility. Your brand's values can attract like-minded customers who might choose you over competitors for these reasons alone.

Testing and feedback are crucial components in developing your brand identity. Survey your audience, gather their thoughts, and be ready to make adjustments. Sometimes, how customers perceive your brand could lead to insights you hadn't considered. Allow your brand to evolve based on genuine customer relationships and feedback.

Remember, your brand extends to every aspect of your business. What happens when there's a customer complaint or an issue with an order? How your business reacts — your actions and communications — is all part of your brand identity. Always act in a manner that reinforces the positive aspects of your brand.

In summary, a memorable brand identity isn't just something you create once and leave be. It's a dynamic, evolving entity that requires attention, creativity, and strategic thinking. In the competitive world of dropshipping, where products can be easily replicated, it's your brand that will provide you with a lasting competitive edge. It's the personality, the story, and the values that customers will come back to, time and time again.

Establishing Trust and Credibility

In the highly competitive world of online dropshipping, building trust and credibility with your audience is imperative for success. Unlike physical stores where customers can touch and feel the products, online shoppers rely on a different set of criteria to assess whether they can trust a vendor. It's the steadiness of these trust signals that can make or break their decision to purchase from your site.

The foundation for establishing trust starts with a professional-looking website. It's often the first point of contact with potential customers, and first impressions count. Ensure your site design is clean, modern, and congruent with your brand identity. An intuitive and secure checkout process is also vital; if customers have even the slightest hesitation about the security of their payment, they're off to a competitor's page.

Transparency is another key element in fostering trust. Be clear about pricing, shipping costs, and return policies. Hidden fees are one of the top reasons for cart abandonment, so being upfront about costs not only reduces that risk but also builds customer confidence in your brand.

Next is the power of social proof. Customer reviews, testimonials, and user-generated content such as photos or videos of your products in use are incredibly persuasive. People trust other consumers over the brand itself. Showcasing positive feedback prominently on your site and social media channels can greatly enhance trust and credibility.

Content is king, not just for SEO, but for establishing expertise in your niche. Crafting informative blog posts, how-to guides, and product-centric content demonstrates knowledge, which translates into trust. Informative content that helps solve problems or answer questions positions your brand as an authority and reliable source.

Building a strong brand voice is also part of establishing credibility. Your tone and style of communication should feel consistent across all platforms, whether it's in the copy on your website, your email newsletters, or your social media posts. A consistent voice helps strengthen brand recognition and fosters a sense of reliability.

Investing in quality customer service is paramount. Quick and helpful responses to inquiries and resolving any issues promptly show that you value your customers and their experience with your brand. Offer multiple channels for customer service, including live chat, email, and phone support, and ensure they are easily accessible.

Utilize seals of trust like SSL certificates to secure your website, demonstrating to customers that you're serious about protecting their data. Displaying badges from trusted payment gateways can also increase confidence for first-time purchasers who might be hesitant to share their credit card details.

To further build credibility, showcase the partnerships with your suppliers. Highlighting their reputability can have a positive rub-off effect on your brand. Position these partnerships as a badge of honor; customers can appreciate the stringent standards you've set for product sourcing.

Maintain a professional online persona. This includes not only your website but also any correspondence and your social media presence. Errors, unprofessional language, or slow response times can all damage a carefully built reputation.

Finally, don't underestimate the importance of consistency. Consistent branding, messaging, posting, product quality, and service all contribute to a consistent brand experience. If customers know what to expect and their expectations are met time and again, trust and loyalty follow suit.

In the realm of dropshipping, where the market is saturated with options, building a brand that exudes trust and credibility can be your untapped competitive advantage. It demands attention to detail, a strategic approach, and a willingness to put in the time and effort needed to cultivate a trustworthy online presence.

Remember that trust is not built overnight. It's earned through each interaction, every transaction, and every fulfilled promise. It's an ongoing commitment to serving the customer's best interest, a commitment that will ultimately pay dividends in the form of loyal, repeat customers and the word-of-mouth marketing they provide for free.

By focusing on trust and credibility, you aren't just creating a brand; you're building a community of followers and customers who believe in you, your products, and your vision. This is how potent branding can elevate a dropshipping business from a simple transactional entity to a trusted name in the digital landscape.

Chapter 8:
Marketing Your Products

Transitioning from the robust foundation established in previous chapters, Chapter 8 delves into propelling your online storefront into the spotlight with strategic marketing approaches. Optimal product visibility hinges on astute marketing tactics in the crowded online marketplace. We'll scrutinize the multifaceted world of digital promotion, guiding you through the labyrinth of social media platforms to ensure your items captivate the right audience. Our focus here is twofold: showcasing your products effectively while maximizing return on investment. This chapter won't detail the intricacies of social media ad crafting, SEO nuance, or email marketing decorum—those are rich subjects for their respective sections. Instead, we'll concentrate on a holistic overview of marketing strategies that elevate your brand's presence and drive sales, deciding which avenues best align with your brand, and the art of weaving compelling narratives around your products that resonate with potential customers. By the chapter's end, you'll discern how to wield marketing analytics like a pro, using data-driven insights to refine your marketing efforts continually and keep your product offerings fresh in the minds of consumers.

Mastering Social Media Advertising

Social media advertising can be the linchpin of a successful online dropshipping business. With billions of potential customers scrolling through their feeds daily, platforms like Facebook, Instagram, Twitter, and Pinterest present a significant opportunity for targeted advertising. The key to effective social media advertising lies in finely-tuned strategies that can convert browsers into buyers.

Understanding different social media platforms is essential before launching your campaigns. Each platform attracts different demographics and behaviors, making it paramount to tailor your approach accordingly. For example, Instagram's visual format is perfect for showcasing products with stunning imagery. However, Twitter might be more effective for sparking conversations and engaging with customers in real time.

Start with defined goals. Are you trying to increase brand awareness, drive traffic to your website, or boost sales? Your objectives will dictate the type of content you create and the metrics you'll use to measure success. If you're aiming for more website visitors, pay attention to click-through rates. For improved sales, conversion rates will be your guide.

An in-depth understanding of your target audience is crucial. Develop personas that represent your potential customers. Take note of their interests, purchasing behavior, and the type of content they engage with. These insights will inform the tone and style of your ads and ensure they resonate with the intended audience.

Creativity in your campaigns sets you apart from the competition. Social media users are bombarded with ads, so it's important that yours catch their attention and spark interest in your products. Videos, user-generated content, and testimonials can be particularly effective in creating an engaging narrative for your brand.

Budgeting effectively is another critical aspect. Social media advertising can quickly become expensive if not managed properly. Set a budget and bid wisely, focusing on ads that yield the best return on investment. It's often a good idea to start small, test different ads, and scale up the ones that perform best.

Retargeting becomes a powerful tool in your arsenal. It allows you to show ads to users who have visited your website but didn't make a purchase. Platforms like Facebook enable advertisers to retarget users based off their onsite behavior, increasing the chances of converting lost prospects into sales.

Utilize A/B testing to refine your social media advertisements. Try different versions of the same ad to see which graphic, headline, or call to action performs better. This constant testing and adapting can lead to incremental improvements in your campaigns' effectiveness.

Tracking and analyzing your advertising data is non-negotiable. Platforms provide a wealth of data, and by analyzing this information, you can make informed decisions to optimize campaigns. Look at the demographics of those interacting with your ads, the times of day when your ads perform best, and which ads lead to actual sales, not just clicks.

Engagement is not just about watching the numbers grow. Once your ads are live, participate in the conversation. Respond to comments, answer messages, and create a community around your brand. Engaged customers are more likely to become repeat customers and even brand advocates.

For a more seamless shopping experience, take advantage of platform shopping features. Instagram and Facebook, for instance, allow users to shop products directly through the app, reducing the number of steps from seeing an ad to making a purchase. Integrating these features can streamline the customer journey and potentially improve conversion rates.

Remember the importance of mobile optimization. With the majority of social media browsing happening on mobile devices, it's crucial to ensure that your ads and landing pages are mobile-friendly. Not doing so can lead to a frustrating user experience and result in lost sales opportunities.

Compliance with advertising policies is also a consideration you can't afford to overlook. Each social media platform has its own set of rules. Familiarize yourself with these guidelines to avoid your ads being rejected, which can disrupt your marketing efforts and delay your campaigns.

In the frenzy of advertising, don't forget about authenticity. Your brand's voice needs to stay true to your values and resonate with your clientele. Social media users value transparency and authenticity, so keep that at the forefront as you design your campaigns.

Finally, never stop learning and adapting. Social media trends and algorithms evolve at lightning speed. Stay informed about the latest features and best practices in social media advertising by following industry leaders, attending webinars, and participating in forums. Keeping up with these changes can give your dropshipping business the competitive edge necessary for e-commerce success.

Harnessing the Power of SEO

Once your dropshipping empire is up and running, diving into the world of Search Engine Optimization (SEO) can be a monumental leap towards perpetual visibility and sales. It's key to understand that SEO isn't just about sprinkling keywords into your content; it's a multifaceted approach to making your online presence more attractive to search engines and, by extension, potential customers. By optimizing your website with relevant keywords, engaging meta descriptions, and quality backlinks, you'll improve your ranking on search engines and drive organic traffic to your site. Be mindful that SEO also demands consistent content creation, such as valuable blog posts that solve your customers' problems, which keeps them returning. Additionally, a mobile-friendly layout and fast loading speeds aren't just user conveniences; they're direct ranking factors in search algorithms. Harnessing SEO effectively ensures that when customers are searching for products you offer, your site is more likely to be the answer to their query, catapulting you ahead of competitors who've overlooked this essential marketing cornerstone.

Email Marketing Do's and Don'ts

In the evolving digital marketplace, email marketing remains a cornerstone strategy for dropshipping entrepreneurs. A well-executed email campaign can drive traffic, enhance customer relationships, and boost sales. However, a poorly handled email strategy can deter potential customers and harm your brand reputation. Here, we'll explore best practices and common pitfalls of email marketing within the context of operating a successful online dropshipping business.

Email marketing begins with building a robust mailing list. It's essential to collect email addresses through legal and ethical means. An effective way to grow your list is by offering incentives to potential subscribers, such as discounts or valuable content. **Do:** provide a clear value proposition for signing up. **Don't:** purchase email lists or add emails without consent, as this can lead to spam complaints and violate privacy laws.

Once you have a mailing list, it's crucial to segment it based on customer behavior or preferences. Personalization can significantly increase open rates and engagement. **Do:** use data-driven insights to tailor your messages. **Don't:** send the same generic email to your entire list, as this often leads to higher unsubscribe rates and lower engagement levels.

The subject line is the first impression your email makes. A compelling subject line can make the difference between an opened email or one that's ignored. **Do:** keep it short, informative, and attention-grabbing. **Don't:** mislead your subscribers with clickbait titles that don't deliver on their promise.

Email content should be relevant and valuable to your audience. Quality content can reinforce trust in your brand and drive sales. **Do:** share helpful information, tips, promotions, and new product announcements. **Don't:** only send out emails when you want to push a sale, as too frequent sales pitches can turn your subscribers off.

Design and layout are pivotal in making your email appealing and easy to navigate. Emails should be visually pleasing and mobile-responsive, as many users check their email on their phones. **Do:** use high-quality images and a clean design. **Don't:** overload your email with too much content or large files that slow down loading times.

Timing and frequency are also key to a successful email campaign. Sending emails at the right time can improve their effectiveness. **Do:** test different times and days to see what works best with your audience. **Don't:** bombard your subscribers' inboxes; too much communication can feel spammy and lead to unsubscribes.

Email marketing is not only for selling but also for engaging with your customers. **Do:** include content that starts conversations and builds community, like surveys or social media links. **Don't:** overlook the importance of building a relationship with your subscribers outside of sales.

Analytics play a role in understanding the success of your campaigns. **Do:** keep an eye on your open rates, click-through rates, and conversions to measure effectiveness. **Don't:** ignore data, as it's a powerful tool in refining your email marketing strategies.

Compliance with email marketing laws, like CAN-SPAM, is non-negotiable. **Do:** ensure that you have permission to email your contacts and that unsubscribe options are clear and functional. **Don't:** forget to follow legal requirements—it can result in heavy fines and damaged credibility.

With email marketing campaigns, testing and optimization are your friends. A/B testing subjects lines, content, and calls to action can provide insights into subscriber preferences. **Do:** use split testing to incrementally improve your emails. **Don't:** get complacent; what worked yesterday might not work today.

Finally, the call to action (CTA) is crucial as it directs your readers to take the desired next step. Whether it's to shop the latest collection or read your newest blog post, the CTA must be clear and compelling. **Do:** use actionable language and place CTAs prominently. **Don't:** leave your subscribers confused about what to do next.

Remember that email marketing should be seen as a dialogue, not a monologue. Encourage feedback and engage with those who respond to your emails. **Do:** invite subscribers to reply with questions or comments. **Don't:** ignore responses—this is an opportunity to deepen customer relationships.

Privacy and respect for personal data should be at the forefront of your email marketing practices. In an age where data breaches are common, assuring your subscribers their data is safe with you is paramount. **Do:** maintain a stringent privacy policy and be transparent about how you use subscriber data. **Don't:** be loose with data management and risk the trust you've built.

Lastly, consistency in your email branding reinforces your dropshipping business's identity. It helps customers instantly recognize your correspondence, building recall and loyalty. **Do:** use consistent branding elements like logos, colors, and tone. **Don't:** vary your branding across emails, as inconsistent branding can confuse subscribers and dilute your business's image.

By following these do's and don'ts, you'll be able to craft email marketing campaigns that engage and convert subscribers, driving your dropshipping business toward greater success. Each email is an opportunity to connect with your audience and strengthen your brand, so invest the time and resources into getting it right.

Chapter 9:
Managing Inventory and Orders

In unison with marketing tactics and brand building, smart handling of inventory and orders serves as the backbone of a flourishing online dropshipping business. This chapter dives into key strategies to keep your operation sailing smoothly, focusing on the intricacies of order fulfillment and inventory control. Effective management is not about eliminating uncertainties—it's about evolving agile practices that allow you to pivot promptly as demand ebbs and flows. You'll learn to employ systems that enable you to monitor stock levels continuously, ensuring products are available when your customers click 'buy.' Additionally, we'll dissect how to enhance the post-order process, fostering customer satisfaction with swift and accurate delivery. It's fundamental to grasp these logistical elements because they make a tangible difference in profitability and customer loyalty. With solid inventory and order management, you're setting up more than just a business; you're crafting an efficient, responsive, customer-centric operation that's built to last.

Streamlining Order Fulfillment

Streamlining order fulfillment is a pivotal component in managing inventory and orders within the dropshipping business model. As order volumes increase, the ability to efficiently process, handle, and ship products becomes critical to maintaining customer satisfaction and operational scalability. In this section, we'll delve into the strategies that can optimize your fulfillment process to ensure your business runs smoothly and customers remain content with their purchasing experience.

First off, it's essential to integrate your shopping cart with your supplier's order fulfillment system. This integration allows for real-time updates on inventory levels, reducing the risk of overselling products that may be out of stock. Furthermore, when a customer places an order, the information can be instantly transmitted to your supplier, slashing the wait-time and accelerating the entire fulfillment cycle.

Another key step in streamlining fulfillment is to choose suppliers with a track record of reliability and speed. Speedy delivery can often be as compelling a selling point as the product itself, so partnering with suppliers who can dispatch orders swiftly and provide tracking information to customers is non-negotiable for a thriving dropshipping business.

Moreover, automating as much of the order processing as possible is vital. Tools that automatically send customers confirmation emails, invoices, and shipping updates not only save time but also enhance the customer experience. Automation in these areas means that you can maintain consistent communication with your customers without having to manually manage each correspondence.

It's also important to maintain accurate product data. This includes dimensions, weight, and any other information that could affect shipping. Accurate data helps in calculating shipping costs accurately and prevents any surprises which could erode your margins or cause customer dissatisfaction due to unexpected fees.

Speaking of shipping, offering multiple shipping options can be a game-changer. Customers appreciate flexibility, so providing a range of choices from standard to express shipping can cater to various needs and urgencies. Just ensure that your margins can support these options, and that you're clear about delivery times for each.

Another aspect to consider is your order fulfillment monitoring system. Keeping an eye on how suppliers are handling the fulfillment process can help you proactively identify and address any issues before they escalate. Regular audits or performance reviews of supplier operations can ensure they're upholding the standards your customers expect.

Training and support are critical as well. Make sure that everyone involved in the order fulfillment process understands their role and how it fits into the larger picture. When your team is knowledgeable, they can help identify efficiency bottlenecks and contribute to process improvements.

Additionally, preparing for peak times is crucial. Known high-volume periods like holidays or promotions require extra planning. Work with your suppliers to anticipate spikes in orders and ensure they have the capacity to handle increased volumes without delays.

Furthermore, don't shy away from leveraging technology such as AI and machine learning, which can forecast demand patterns, optimize delivery routes, and even automate customer support. This progressive approach can lead to significant improvements in fulfilling orders accurately and promptly.

It's also beneficial to establish a clear returns policy and process. This sets customer expectations and can streamline the return process for both you and your customer. Having an efficient system in place can simplify the tracking and management of returned items, reducing the time and cost associated with handling returns.

Conversely, minimizing returns is just as important as managing them. This can be achieved by providing in-depth product descriptions, accurate images, and reviews to help customers make informed decisions. Fewer returns mean a more efficient fulfillment process and higher overall customer satisfaction.

Fostering open communication with your suppliers can't be overstated. Regularly touching base with them about their fulfillment process can bring insights that can lead to improvements. It's a symbiotic relationship; your success is their success and vice versa.

Lastly, always keep the end-game in focus: the customer's satisfaction. Streamlining your fulfillment process should ultimately lead to a better customer experience. Regardless of how efficient your process is internally, if your customers are unhappy, it's time to reevaluate and adjust your approach.

In summary, streamlining order fulfillment demands a combination of strategy, technology, and strong partnerships with suppliers. Tackling it head-on will significantly contribute to a smoother running business, bolstering your reputation and, ultimately, your bottom line. Keep refining and improving your process, staying agile to adapt to changes in customer expectations, market demands, and new technologies. And this way, you keep marching towards establishing your dropshipping business as a paragon of efficiency and customer satisfaction.

Inventory Management Best Practices

Efficiently managing inventory is the cornerstone of a profitable dropshipping business. A superior inventory management system keeps your operations running smoothly and ensures that customer satisfaction remains high. Let's delve into the best practices that can safeguard your business against inventory mishaps and improve your bottom line.

Firstly, understand the importance of data accuracy. Accurate data cannot be compromised when managing inventory. Ensuring that your stock levels are reflected correctly across all platforms prevents overselling and stockouts. Utilize inventory management software that syncs with your sales channels to update information in real-time. This integration is crucial for maintaining a clear picture of your stock levels at all times.

Regularly reviewing your inventory performance is critical. Analyze sales data, stock levels, and customer demand to understand which products are your top performers and which aren't meeting expectations. This will help you make informed decisions about restocking and streamlining your product offerings.

Anticipate demand to avoid stockouts, which can be detrimental to your reputation and sales. Pay attention to your sales trends and any external factors that may cause a surge in demand. Having a strategy to manage these fluctuations—such as keeping a buffer stock or working with suppliers who can quickly fulfill orders—is essential.

Equally necessary is building strong relationships with your suppliers. A trustworthy and proactive supplier can make all the difference in addressing unexpected shortages and meeting client demands swiftly. Keep communication open and understand their lead times to better plan your inventory requirements.

Inventory management is not just about numbers; it's also about ensuring product quality. Regular quality checks can prevent customer dissatisfaction and returns, which can erode your profits and damage your brand reputation.

Another valuable practice is setting clear inventory KPIs (Key Performance Indicators). Tracking metrics such as inventory turnover, carrying cost, and order accuracy can help you measure the health of your inventory management process and identify areas for improvement.

Implementing just-in-time (JIT) inventory strategies can reduce the costs associated with holding stock. By receiving goods only as they are needed in the production process, you minimize the amount of inventory you need to keep on hand, reducing storage and insurance costs.

Don't forget the significance of contingency planning. In dropshipping, many factors are beyond your control. Having a contingency plan in place for dealing with stockouts, supplier issues, or shipping delays is critical so that you can act quickly to resolve issues.

Also, consider the benefits of automating inventory tasks. Automation can eliminate manual data entry, reduce human errors, and save time. Setting up auto-replenish thresholds for your best-selling items can ensure you never miss a sales opportunity.

Keep your inventory lean by practicing SKU rationalization. The rationale behind this is to keep only profitable products that align with your target market's preferences. Eliminating underperforming SKUs helps reduce waste and optimize storage space.

Embrace demand forecasting tools and techniques. Modern inventory management software comes equipped with tools that can predict future sales based on historical data, trends, and seasonal fluctuations. Integrating these tools into your strategy can guide your stock replenishing decisions effectively.

Inventory shrinkage due to theft, damage, or administrative errors is also important to monitor. Regularly conduct audits and reconcile physical inventory with your records to avoid discrepancies that can impact your bottom line.

Lastly, it's worth investing in training for your team. Make sure they understand the tools and processes that your inventory system employs. Educated and knowledgeable teams can better manage inventory and respond to complex scenarios with greater confidence.

Adopting these inventory management best practices should lead to improved stock control, a more streamlined operation, and, ultimately, heightened customer satisfaction. As you fortify your inventory management, your dropshipping business is poised to reap increased profitability and greater resilience against the challenges of the ecommerce arena.

Chapter 10:
Seasonal Sales and Product Trends

The cyclical ebb and flow of consumer demand are at the heart of successfully navigating seasonal sales and harnessing product trends in the dropshipping world. Understanding the nuances of seasonal variations can elevate your strategy from simply reacting to the market to proactively shaping your sales approach. With the shift in seasons comes an opportunity to capitalize on the specific needs and wants of customers: from outdoor gear in summer to cozy home decor in the cold months. To stay ahead, you'll want to monitor upcoming holidays, events, and changing consumer behavior patterns. This vigilance allows you to tailor your inventory and marketing efforts, ensuring that your product offerings resonate with the seasonal sentiment. By skillfully adapting your product line and marketing campaigns to these shifting trends, you can enhance customer engagement, boost sales, and maintain a competitive edge all year round.

Leveraging Seasonality in Your Sales Strategy

An integral component of driving sales in your online dropshipping business lies in understanding and capitalizing on seasonal trends. Seasonality refers to periodic fluctuations that regularly occur in a specific season, month, or even week, impacting consumer behavior and sales. By tailoring your sales strategy to align with these fluctuations, you can maximize both revenue and customer engagement.

Start by identifying key sales periods relevant to your niche. For instance, a dropshipping store specializing in outdoor gear will anticipate a surge in sales in the months leading to summer when camping and hiking are at their peak. Knowing this, you'd stock up on relevant inventory and increase your marketing efforts accordingly. The key to success here is anticipation and preparedness.

But seasonality isn't just about adjusting to busy periods; it's also about using the quieter times to your advantage. During off-peak seasons, you can focus on building customer relationships, gathering feedback, and improving your store. This ensures you are well-equipped to meet your customers' needs when peak season rolls around again.

Moreover, holidays such as Black Friday, Cyber Monday, Christmas, and even back-to-school season can massively impact sales. Developing a marketing calendar that aligns with these holidays allows you to create promotions and marketing campaigns that cater specifically to the increased demand.

A vital aspect of leveraging seasonality is adjusting your inventory accordingly. You don't want to be stuck with unsold, seasonal items once their demand wanes, so planning your stock levels and leveraging pre-order options can be incredibly efficient ways to manage inventory risks.

Seasonal pricing adjustments can also be an effective strategy. Dynamically pricing your products in response to demand can help you stay competitive and increase sales during peak times, while discounting stock before the season ends might reduce losses on remaining inventory.

Creating seasonal bundles or packages is another way to boost sales during peak seasons. Grouping complementary products together at a discounted rate can entice customers to make larger purchases, leveraging the increased willingness to spend during these periods.

It's also crucial to use season-specific marketing messages. Tailoring your ad copy and imagery to resonate with the mood of the season can improve connection with your target audience. For instance, cozy scenes during the winter holidays or vibrant beach settings for summer can put customers in the right frame of mind to purchase.

Don't forget about email marketing in your seasonal strategy. Sending themed newsletters that align with upcoming holidays or seasons keeps your audience informed of offers and encourages repeat business. Personalizing your emails based on previous purchases can also drive sales by reminding customers of products they are likely interested in.

Utilizing social media platforms to run time-bound campaigns can generate buzz and drive sales. Platforms like Instagram and Facebook are ideal for creating visually appealing content that can go viral, providing a widespread promotion with minimal cost.

Investing in seasonal SEO can also lead to a significant boost in organic traffic. Create content and optimize keywords for upcoming seasons or holidays well in advance. This ensures that when the season is at its peak, your store appears at the top of search results for season-related queries.

Analytics are your best friend when planning for seasonality. Review your sales data from previous years to understand patterns and consumer behavior. This data will help you forecast demand, set realistic goals, and craft a strategy that aligns with consumer trends.

For those new to the dropshipping game, it's vital to start small with seasonality. Choose one or two key seasons or holidays to focus on initially, and as you gain more experience, expand your efforts to cover more seasonal opportunities.

Last but not least, engage with your customers post-season. Gather feedback on your seasonal promotions and strategies to learn what worked and what didn't. This information is invaluable for refining your approach for the next season.

In conclusion, effectively leveraging seasonality in your sales strategy requires a combination of preparation, timely marketing, inventory management, and ongoing analysis. By understanding the ebb and flow of consumer demand throughout the year, you can position your dropshipping business to make the most of high-impact selling opportunities while maintaining stability during quieter times.

Predicting and Acting on Product Trends

As we delve further into the world of dropshipping, it's evident that staying ahead of product trends isn't just beneficial; it's essential for survival. Especially within the context of seasonal sales, predicting and capitalizing on these trends can make the difference between an average quarter and a record-breaking one. Knowing which products are likely to catch consumer interest helps anticipate demand and ensure your offerings remain fresh and relevant.

To effectively predict product trends, it's crucial to develop a keen sense of market awareness. This involves not only paying attention to the ebb and flow of consumer interests but also actively researching and utilizing various tools and resources that can provide insights into upcoming trends. For instance, Google Trends is a potent tool that allows you to see what people are searching for and how those trends are changing over time.

Another aspect of trend forecasting is understanding cultural shifts and global events. Holiday seasons, for instance, have a predictable impact on certain product categories like decorations, gifts, and seasonal attire. However, trends can also be driven by unforeseen factors like a viral social media post, a new mobile app, or even news events. Being quick to identify these trends as they emerge can position your dropshipping business at the forefront of the curve.

Acting on trends requires agility—not just in your thinking, but in your operational capabilities as well. This means establishing a supply chain that's flexible and responsive. Build a good relationship with suppliers so that when a trend takes off, you're able to stock up quickly without getting stuck with excess inventory if the demand wanes.

It's essential to realize that trends can vary significantly depending on your target market. Demographic data is invaluable for predicting which products will resonate with your audience. A product trending with teenagers, for example, may not hold the same appeal for baby boomers. Holistic market research that combines demographic segmentation with trend analysis will serve as a guiding light for your product selection.

Seasonal trends can be particularly predictable when it comes to certain categories like apparel, which changes with the seasons. However, there's always room for surprises, which is why it's critical to monitor sales data closely. This will help you spot any gradual changes in what your customers are buying so you can adjust your inventory accordingly.

While predicting trends might occasionally feel like staring into a crystal ball, the use of data analytics and AI-driven insights has made it less of guesswork. These technologies enable dropshippers to assess large volumes of data for predictive patterns that can inform on potential hits or duds.

The key to successful trend prediction lies as much in timing as it does in accuracy. It's not just about having the right product; it's about having it at the right time. Forecasting methods should therefore integrate historical sales data to pinpoint not only what will trend but when it's likely to do so.

Marketing also plays a significant role in capitalizing on trends. Once you've identified a trending product, you need to communicate its availability to your potential customers. Here, social media and email marketing can be powerful tools for promoting these products to your audience, especially if you're able to deliver the message with a sense of urgency and exclusivity.

However, it's equally important to maintain a level of flexibility in your marketing strategy. Trends can be fleeting, and what is popular one week may not be the next. Stay prepared to pivot your advertising focus swiftly to avoid being left with unsellable stock.

It's also worth noting that not every trending product will fit within your brand's niche or ethos. It can be tempting to jump on every popular item, but doing so recklessly can dilute your brand and create confusion among your customers. Select trends that align with your brand identity and meet your profitability goals.

Dropshippers should also be mindful of the balance between jumping on trends and creating them. While the former involves less risk, the latter can yield greater rewards. By establishing yourself as a trendsetter within your niche, you can garner a following of customers who look to your store for the next big thing.

Ultimately, capitalizing on product trends is part art, part science. The art is in reading the cultural zeitgeist and interpreting it within the context of your niche. The science is in the data analysis, the meticulous research, and the methodical approach to responsive supply chain management. It's a delicate balance, but when done correctly, it can lead to a thriving online business.

In conclusion, predicting and acting on product trends is about staying informed, being nimble, and making calculated decisions. While some trends may come and go with the changing seasons, your ability to adapt will determine the enduring success of your dropshipping empire.

As we close this section and move into the nitty-gritty of customer service in the next, remember that trends are also shaped by how people feel about the products and the service they receive. An excellent product trend paired with outstanding customer service can multiply its success manifold. So, while you're keeping an eye on the pulse of market trends, don't lose sight of the customer experience that supports it.

Chapter 11:
Customer Service Excellence

In the swiftly turning world of online dropshipping, customer service isn't just a support function—it's a cornerstone of business success. We've meandered through the intricacies of setting up a stellar online presence, from the delicate choices of niche selection to the calculated crafting of a seamless sales funnel. Now, it's time to delve into the art of customer service excellence, the very heartbeat of a flourishing dropshipping venture. Exceptional service not only adds a personal touch to the virtual shopping experience but also builds a formidable wall of loyalty that competitors can't easily breach. It's about grasping the pulse of customer satisfaction, embracing every complaint as a golden chance to shine, and turning potential returns into opportunities for reinforcement of commitment. Prepare to explore the strategies that transform passive interactions into active relationships, fortifying your brand as one that customers won't hesitate to return to, time and time again.

Understanding the Importance of Customer Satisfaction

As we delve into the realm of customer service excellence in the flourishing industry of online dropshipping, understanding the significance of customer satisfaction becomes critical. Operators of online businesses must prioritize customer satisfaction to ensure longevity and profitability. Satisfied customers represent the foundation upon which the credibility and success of a dropshipping venture are built.

To appreciate why customer satisfaction holds such weight, it's essential to recognize its impact on repeat business. When customers are pleased with their purchasing experience, they are more likely to become loyal patrons. This loyalty not simply translates to return purchases but often leads to customers becoming advocates for your brand, providing invaluable word-of-mouth marketing.

The impact of customer satisfaction extends to feedback and reviews, which can make or break an online business. Positive reviews left by satisfied customers act as powerful testimonials that can attract new customers, while negative feedback can substantially dent a brand's reputation and deter potential customers from engaging with the business.

Engagement and community building are also crucial aspects influenced by customer satisfaction. In an online landscape where personal touch is often lacking, creating a community around your brand can give your business an edge. Customer satisfaction can foster an environment where customers feel heard and valued, thus establishing a community that supports and promotes your brand.

Financially, the cost of acquiring new customers is significantly higher than retaining existing ones. Customer satisfaction plays a pivotal role in customer retention, and by focusing on keeping your current customers happy, you're likely to see a decrease in marketing costs and a rise in profits.

Moreover, customer satisfaction drives brand differentiation. In a marketplace crowded with similar offerings, a high level of customer service can differentiate your dropshipping business and provide a competitive advantage. This differentiation is often what prompts a shopper to choose your brand over another.

Data gathered from satisfied customers can reveal powerful insights into user experience, preferences, and possible product improvements. Armed with this information, a business can make informed decisions to enhance operations and tailor the customer experience to meet and exceed customer expectations.

As the dropshipping model inherently deals with third-party suppliers, ensuring that customer satisfaction is not compromised due to shipping and handling becomes even more significant. A single bad experience related to a delayed delivery or damaged product can lead to dissatisfaction, making it imperative to collaborate closely with reliable suppliers.

It's important to remember that customer satisfaction also correlates with a reduced rate of returns and complaints. When customers are content with their purchase, they're less inclined to return items, lowering the logistical and administrative burdens associated with returns processing.

Customer satisfaction is not a finite element but a continuous goal. Businesses must keep abreast of customer preferences and shifting market trends to continuously adapt and deliver the experience that meets, if not exceeds, customer expectations. This requires an ongoing commitment to learning from customer feedback and implementing changes accordingly.

Given the nature of online interactions, any dissatisfaction can quickly become amplified through social media and review sites. An unsatisfied customer has the tools to broadcast their displeasure to a large audience. Thus, focusing on customer satisfaction is also a defensive strategy against potential reputational damage.

Creating a satisfaction-centric culture among your staff and any third parties you work with is paramount. Educating and training everyone involved in your dropshipping business about the importance of customer satisfaction will ensure that your operational practices and customer service policies remain customer-focused.

Additionally, customer satisfaction can be regarded as a barometer for a business's health. A declining satisfaction rate can often be an early indicator of underlying issues that need swift attention. Agile responsiveness to these changes not only addresses the immediate concerns but also showcases to customers a commitment to their satisfaction.

To conclude, the reason customer satisfaction is imperative in the online dropshipping ecosystem is that it serves as the heartbeat of your business. It permeates through every facet of your operations and ultimately dictates the trajectory of your enterprise. By placing the happiness of your customers at the forefront of your actions, you lay the groundwork for a successful and enduring dropshipping empire.

Your end goal, as an online entrepreneur, should always involve fostering a seamless and satisfying experience that resonates with your customers. By doing so, you don't just sell products; you craft experiences, build relationships, and encourage a loyalty that transcends the usual vendor-customer dynamic. In the end, customer satisfaction is the linchpin that holds together the vast machine of your online dropshipping business, propelling it towards success and sustainability in the competitive digital marketplace.

Handling Complaints and Returns Gracefully

In any business, particularly in online dropshipping, the way you handle complaints and returns can significantly impact your reputation and, ultimately, your success. As you may already understand, achieving customer service excellence is vital. Let's dive into how you can manage these delicate situations with poise and professionalism.

When a customer approaches you with a complaint, the initial step is to listen actively. Make sure they feel heard and understood. Acknowledge the inconvenience they've experienced, and thank them for bringing the issue to your attention. It's essential to remain calm and collected, avoiding any defensive stance that could escalate the situation.

After understanding the complaint, it's crucial to investigate promptly. Determine whether the issue is a one-time mistake or a recurring problem that needs a more strategic fix. By doing so, you're not just solving an individual problem but preventing future complaints.

An effective complaint resolution process should have clear guidelines. Establish and communicate the steps you will take to resolve the issue. This can include providing a replacement, refund, or other compensatory measures. Customers appreciate transparency, so keep them informed about the progress of their complaint resolution.

In cases where returns are a necessary course of action, streamline the process for your customers. Make clear your return policy on your website and ensure it's both fair and competitive. Implementing a hassle-free return system not only caters to customer convenience but also builds trust.

Your attitude towards returns should be as flexible as your business model allows. Even if it means accepting the return of a perfectly functional product, the long-term gains in customer loyalty and word-of-mouth could outweigh the short-term losses. You want your customers to feel assured that their satisfaction is paramount.

Quite often, complaints and returns are opportunities in disguise – opportunities to learn and enhance your offerings. Debrief and discuss with your team or suppliers about what might have gone wrong and how such issues can be mitigated. Use the feedback to improve product quality or update your website's product descriptions for accuracy.

Remember, compensation isn't always monetary. Sometimes, a sincere apology and a discount on future purchases can go a long way in mending fences. Personalized responses to complaints show that you value your customers as individuals.

Train your customer service team extensively to handle complaints and manage returns effectively. Your team should empathize with customers, convey the right tone in communications, and be empowered to make decisions that will resolve situations quickly.

Tracking complaints and analyzing them can reveal patterns that, once addressed, could lead to significant improvements in your business operations. Consider establishing metrics — such as the number of complaints resolved within a day — as a part of your customer service KPIs.

Automation tools can be employed to streamline the returns process. However, ensure that they don't depersonalize the experience. Customers should still feel they can reach out to a human who understands their problems and is willing to help.

Online reviews are not to be overlooked. Monitor what customers say about your handling of their complaints and returns. Constructive responses to negative reviews can turn an unhappy customer into a loyal one and show potential customers that you're committed to customer satisfaction.

In addition to this, foster a company culture that values customer feedback. Each complaint or return carries with it a lesson on how to better your service. Cultivating this culture encourages continuous improvement and sets you apart in the competitive dropshipping market.

Lastly, it's worthwhile to look at how you can minimize the likelihood of complaints and returns. Maybe it's offering better product descriptions, clearer images, more precise shipping details, or a more straightforward website navigation. Prevention is, after all, better than cure.

Handling complaints and returns with grace is not just about salvaging a transaction — it's about nurturing relationships. Those online entrepreneurs who master this aspect of customer service are the ones who truly thrive. They understand that ultimate satisfaction for both parties is not merely a transactional end but a stepping stone to a loyal customer base.

Chapter 12:
Scaling Your Business

Now that you've laid the groundwork for your online dropshipping business by carving out a niche, sourcing products, and refining your sales funnels, it's time to turn your attention to growth. Scaling your business is the natural next step, requiring strategic thinking and a keen eye for the right timing. In this chapter, we'll explore the intricacies of measuring your business's readiness to scale, identifying the indicators that signal expansion viability, and the methods to do so responsibly without overextending your resources. Expanding a business isn't just about pushing sales; it's a multifaceted endeavor that encompasses advancing your marketing efforts, solidifying your supply chain, and enhancing your customer support—all while maintaining the quality of your service and managing the increased operational complexity. Here, you'll learn to anticipate the challenges that scaling brings and tackle them head-on, ensuring that your growth is sustainable and your business's foundation remains solid, even as you reach for new heights in the competitive dropshipping arena.

When and How to Scale

Scaling your business isn't just about growth for growth's sake; it's about expanding wisely and sustainably. In the dynamic world of online dropshipping, recognizing the right time to scale is as crucial as knowing how to do it. It is that pivotal point where demand begins to outpace your current capabilities. When customer inquiries come flooding in, inventory turnover is swift, and metrics show steady profitability, it's time to consider scaling.

Discerning when to scale involves analyzing your business data closely. Are you consistently hitting your sales targets? Is there a stable upward trajectory in your web traffic? If you're seeing a surge that isn't just a fleeting spike due to seasonal changes, and your infrastructure is struggling to keep up, scaling becomes imperative.

But it's not just about the numbers. An often overlooked aspect of scaling is customer feedback. If your customer base is expanding and the satisfaction rate is high, consider this a clear signal that your market is ready for you to escalate your operations. In the end, retention and customer lifetime value are strong indicators of your business's potential to grow.

Once you've determined it's time to scale, one of the first steps is to enhance your technological foundation. If your website is struggling with the current load, it will only buckle under the added strain of growth. Ensuring that your hosting service can handle increased traffic and transactions is paramount. Investing in scalable cloud services or a dedicated server might be prudent before pushing for growth.

Upgrading your e-commerce platform to one that can effortlessly manage a higher volume of sales while providing a seamless customer experience is also essential. Remember, a platform breakdown during a time of rapid growth can lead to lost sales and, more importantly, lost trust.

Expanding your product offerings could be another dimension of scaling, but caution is the watchword here. Don't just add new products for the sake of variety. Instead, carry out a detailed analysis to understand what additional items or variations your customers are clamoring for. Dive deep into market trends and consumer behavior to identify profitable additions to your catalog.

Efficient inventory management becomes even more critical when you scale. While you might not store products in a traditional sense with dropshipping, staying on top of stock levels with your suppliers prevents backorders and dissatisfaction. Scaling up might mean negotiating new deals with current suppliers or bringing additional suppliers into the fold to ensure product availability keeps pace with demand.

Consider automating as many processes as possible. Automation in order processing and customer service can streamline operations and allow you to handle a larger volume of transactions effectively. Software tools that can help with automation range from customer relationship management to inventory tracking systems.

Logistics is another area to scrutinize. As you grow, you'll need to maintain or even improve delivery times, making it necessary to evaluate your shipping arrangements. Work closely with logistical partners who can scale such as couriers and postal services—to ensure that increased order volumes won't lead to slowdowns or errors.

Scaling your dropshipping operation also involves scaling your marketing efforts. What worked when you were smaller may not be as effective at a larger scale. Allocate a larger budget to your most successful channels but remember to maintain a diversified marketing strategy to not become dependent on a single source of leads or revenue.

Scaling won't work without the right team. If you've been flying solo or with a small team, hiring might be necessary. Identify the competencies and roles that will support your growth—such as customer service reps, marketing experts, and administrative support.

Seasoned professionals can be game-changers for scaling your online business.

Outsourcing can be an alternative to hiring full-time staff, especially for tasks that are necessary but not central to your core competencies. From social media management to virtual assistance, outsourcing can offer the expertise needed without the commitment of in-house staff.

Lastly, implementing a robust customer support system will ensure that your quality of service doesn't deteriorate as you grow. You must continue to collect feedback, resolve issues promptly, and provide a personal touch that makes customers feel valued—even as order volumes soar.

To sum up, scaling requires careful preparation, strategic investment, and a systematized approach. It's about doing more of what works and constantly refining your operations to serve an expanding customer base efficiently. Keep a steadfast eye on the quality of service and customer satisfaction as these are the true barometers of successful scaling. Growing your online dropshipping business isn't just about expanding your footprint; it's about sustaining momentum while ensuring each step adds value to your brand and your customers.

As you venture into the next chapters, you'll get into the nitty-gritty of hiring effectively and navigating the outsourcing landscape. Remember, successful scaling is a compound effect of strategic decisions and optimized systems working harmoniously to take your business to new heights.

Hiring and Outsourcing Effectively

In the journey of scaling your dropshipping business, there will come an intersection where growth hinges not solely on your personal effort but on the strategic expansion of your team. Your initiatives will outgrow the confines of a one-person operation, and you'll need to navigate the complexities of hiring and outsourcing to maximize your enterprise's potential.

Before posting your first job opening or reaching out to contractors, it's imperative to have a crystal-clear understanding of your business needs. Evaluate the areas where additional hands could translate directly to greater revenue or improved customer experiences. Perhaps your customer support needs fortification, or maybe managing your growing inventory has become a herculean task.

Outsourcing may be a suitable path for certain facets of your business. Administration, accounting, or digital marketing might be better handled by third-party experts, especially if these are not your strong suits. Outsourcing these tasks can free up your time to focus on strategy and growth while benefiting from the expertise of professionals who have the infrastructure and knowledge base to perform effectively.

As you consider hiring, focus on roles that demand ongoing attention within your business. A dedicated customer service representative or a savvy social media manager can add immense long-term value. When hiring, seek individuals whose skills align with your core business goals and who demonstrate a capacity for growth and adaptation.

The remote nature of online dropshipping businesses allows you to tap into a global pool of talent. This flexibility can be advantageous as you source for the best fit regardless of geographical constraints. Utilize online job platforms where you can find skilled freelancers or full-time candidates with the specific set of skills you require.

During the hiring process, clarity in your job descriptions and expectations is crucial. Definitive roles and clear deliverables help in attracting the right candidates and setting the stage for future performance reviews. Be as specific as possible about the skills and duties involved, and consider including information about your company culture and values to attract individuals who will mesh well with your business's ethos.

When engaging with freelancers or outsourcing agencies, it's important to construct detailed contracts specifying the scope of work, timelines, deliverables, and payment terms. These agreements not only protect your business but also provide security for the provider, fostering a solid and trusting relationship.

Implement systems, like project management software, that facilitate collaboration and communication with your new team members. Whether they're down the street or across the globe, these tools ensure that everyone stays on the same page, deadlines are met, and productivity is tracked.

Bringing on new hires also means dedicating time for effective onboarding. Ensure they understand not only their roles but also how their work impacts the bigger picture. Provide them with the resources they need to quickly become effective members of your team, and consider a mentorship program where they can learn the nuances of your business from seasoned team members.

Don't neglect the importance of company culture, even in a virtual environment. Creating a strong sense of team and company identity can boost morale, foster loyalty, and result in higher productivity. Regular virtual meetups, team-building exercises, and open communication channels contribute to a positive work atmosphere.

Performance monitoring should be an ongoing task. Set periodic evaluations to review the work quality and the achievement of set goals. This enables you to provide feedback and address any potential issues before they become major obstacles. Also, recognize and reward outstanding work to motivate your team and encourage high performance.

Looking at the long-term sustainability, training and developing your team should be part of your strategy. Investing in their growth is an investment in your business's future. Training can include anything from specific job skills to broader topics like customer service, leadership, and time management.

For tasks requiring specialized knowledge or experience, like legal compliance or tax planning, always consider professional services. As your dropshipping business grows, the complexity of these issues typically increases, making professional assistance not just helpful but essential for maintaining proper business operation and avoiding costly mistakes.

Lastly, be prepared to revisit and refine your hiring and outsourcing strategies regularly. As your business scales, so will your needs and the skillsets required to support that growth. Keep a pulse on the effectiveness of your team and make adjustments as the market and your business model evolve.

When executed properly, hiring and outsourcing can propel your dropshipping business to new heights. It's about finding the right balance of in-house talent and outsourced expertise to streamline operations, enhance your offerings, and secure a dominant place in the competitive online marketplace.

Chapter 13:
Turning Your Keyboard Into Cash

As we wrap up our exploration of creating a booming dropshipping business, it's clear that the journey from conceptualizing your brand to realizing your entrepreneurial dreams is encapsulated in the keystrokes that brought your vision to life. In this conclusion, we encapsulate the exhilaration of transforming an everyday object—a keyboard—into a tool that unlocks the treasure trove of online commerce.

Throughout this book, we've seen how plugging into the dropshipping model affords flexibility, scalability, and access to a global market without the heavy baggage of inventory management. By now, you've learned to navigate the intricate dropshipping terrain, from selecting products to aligning with credible suppliers, setting competitive prices, and developing sales strategies that resonate with your target audience.

The internet has democratized entrepreneurship, providing platforms where setting up your shop is just a few clicks away. Crafting your online presence, the very first step, is not just about aesthetic appeal, but also about establishing a robust, conversion-oriented platform. This is where the commitment in each keystroke plants the seeds of future sales.

Identifying your niche isn't just a task; it's an ongoing conversation between market trends, consumer behavior, and your brand voice. The uniqueness of your approach in this crowded market will, in many ways, dictate your success. Thus, it's here that we've spent considerable time understanding how to carve out a space that's uniquely yours.

Finding the balance between demand and supply as it pertains to product sourcing is like conducting an orchestra. Each section—be it the brass, woodwinds, or strings—needs to come in at the right time. Similarly, you juggle supplier relationships and market needs to create a symphony of retail harmony.

Creating an attractive pricing strategy can be likened to setting the right tempo. Too fast, and you may not sustain the pace; too slow, and the market might outpace you. This delicate balance ensures that you remain competitive without thinning your margins to the breaking point.

Your sales funnel is the pathway that leads customers from awareness to purchase, and crafting this carefully is akin to penning a compelling narrative. The combination of high-converting landing pages and strategic upsells can set the stage for a profitable long-term relationship with your customers.

In the realm of e-commerce, Branding is the personality behind your products, a vital factor in customer retention and attraction. Establishing trust and credibility goes beyond the superficial, requiring a keen sense of consistency and an unwavering commitment to your brand's values and promises.

Through the chapters on marketing, you've learned that there's a finesse to reaching out to potential customers. Leveraging platforms like social media, maximizing SEO, and sending out engaging emails are the modern equivalents of an enthralling sales pitch. Your keyboard becomes a channel, streaming your message into the hearts and screens of your audience.

While abundance is a sign of success, managing this plenty is an art. Streamlining order fulfillment and managing inventory are back-end tasks that support the front-end spectacle of sales and marketing. They must function seamlessly to create a sustainable model—a nod to the logistical symphony working behind the scenes.

Just like fashion trends, seasonality in sales can dictate the ebb and flow of your business. Staying ahead of these trends can directly impact your bottom line, and making sure you're aligned with customer demands ensures your products don't linger in the limbo of an outdated inventory graveyard.

Exceptional customer service is no longer a nice-to-have but a necessity in a consumer-centric landscape. It reflects the ethos of your enterprise and determines the loyalty and satisfaction of your customer. It is here that you're not just typing responses, but crafting experiences that resonate with empathy and professionalism.

Eventually, growth becomes the inevitable pursuit, but knowing when and how to scale is crucial. Expansion requires a symphony of strategic hiring, the tuning of processes, and sometimes, the courage to pivot. Your keyboard, in essence, becomes a commanding tool that orchestrates this next phase of your business journey.

Your keyboard, once a mere peripheral, is now your wand yielding the power to incite commerce, spark connections, and build empires. We hope that the chapters preceding have equipped you with the knowledge to confidently navigate the dropshipping realm, tapping into its potential, and turning it into a source of revenue and fulfillment.

As we conclude, remember that success is not only measured by profit but by the satisfaction derived from building something from the ground up. Your keyboard has given you access to a world of opportunity; it's now up to you to type your way to triumph. May each key you press bring you closer to the success you envision, transforming your efforts into a prosperous online dropshipping business.

Appendix A:
Dropshipping Resource Directory

As you've moved through the various chapters of this guide, you've gained a wealth of knowledge on starting a dropshipping business, from clarifying your business model to refining your sales funnel. But even with all the strategy and insight, the right resources are crucial for turning those well-laid plans into action. Compiled here in Appendix A is a treasure trove of hand-picked tools, platforms, and services that'll support you in your dropshipping journey. Let's dive in.

1. Product Research Tools

- **Google Trends:** A free tool that tracks search query popularity, an invaluable asset for identifying market interests.
- **Jungle Scout:** A comprehensive service for product research, especially useful for Amazon dropshippers.
- **Oberlo:** This platform assists in finding products to sell and directly integrates with Shopify stores.

2. Supplier Directories

- **Alibaba:** The behemoth supplier directory for sourcing products in bulk, often from manufacturers based in Asia.
- **SaleHoo:** A curated supplier directory that connects dropshippers with reputable wholesalers worldwide.

3. E-commerce Platforms

1. **Shopify:** One of the most user-friendly e-commerce platforms with powerful dropshipping integrations.

2. **WooCommerce:** A flexible open-source solution, perfect for those who are familiar with WordPress.

3. **BigCommerce:** A robust platform that scales with your growth, great for more tech-savvy entrepreneurs.

4. Hosting Services

- **Bluehost:** Recommended for its strong uptime and customer support, ideal for WordPress-based shops.

- **SiteGround:** Known for its high-performance hosting and e-commerce friendly services.

5. Payment Gateways

1. **PayPal:** A widely accepted payment gateway with buyer and seller protection policies.

2. **Stripe:** A well-regarded option for its clear pricing and ease of integration.

6. Marketing and SEO Tools

- **Google Ads:** For running paid advertising campaigns targeting specific keywords.

- **Mailchimp:** An email marketing service that's perfect for those getting started with email campaigns.

- **Ahrefs:** A toolset for SEO and marketing, including keyword research and site audits.

7. Customer Service Management

- **ZenDesk:** Provides a comprehensive suite for managing customer support with scalability.
- **Freshdesk:** A good choice for new dropshippers desiring a simpler, effective customer service tool.

8. Analytics and Data Analysis

- **Google Analytics:** An indispensable free tool for monitoring and understanding your website traffic.
- **Hotjar:** Offers heat maps and behavior analytics to optimize your user experience and conversion rates.

Of course, no directory can cover absolutely every tool you might discover or need on your entrepreneurial path. Yet, this roundup gives a solid foundation of quality resources that have been proven to work for countless dropshipping professionals. Your ideal toolkit may evolve as you grow, but these resources will get you started on the right foot. Use them to build, optimize, and scale your business efficiently and effectively.

Navigate these resources with your strategic goals in mind and remember that the best tools are the ones that align with your unique business needs. With this directory, you're well on your way to turning your dropshipping business from a blueprint into a booming digital empire.

Appendix B:
Legal Considerations and Documents

Introduction to Legal Foundations

Establishing a dropshipping business isn't just about finding the right products and building an engaging website; it's crucial to understand the legal framework that underpins your operations. This involves navigating through various statutory requirements and ensuring that all the necessary documents are in place to legitimize your business activities and protect against liabilities.

Business Structure and Registration

One of the first decisions you'll face is choosing the appropriate business structure for your online enterprise. Will you operate as a sole proprietor, form a partnership, or incorporate as an LLC or corporation? Each has distinct implications for liability, taxes, and ongoing compliance requirements. Registering your business with the state and obtaining an Employer Identification Number (EIN) from the Internal Revenue Service (IRS) are critical steps in legitimizing your enterprise.

Reseller Permits and Licenses

Depending on your location and the nature of the products you're selling, you might need a reseller's permit or a business license. These documents allow you to purchase goods from suppliers without paying sales tax and collect sales tax from customers in your state. Pay attention to the specific rules and regulations of your state and local government, as requirements can vary widely.

Understanding Dropshipping Agreements

Your relationship with suppliers is key to your business success. You'll likely need to sign dropshipping agreements that dictate the terms of your partnership. These documents should cover order fulfillment responsibilities, payment terms, and how to handle returns or damaged goods. It's essential to have a clear understanding of these agreements to manage expectations and ensure a smooth operation.

E-Commerce Legalities

Operating online introduces additional considerations like privacy policies, terms of service, and electronic communication compliance. Ensure that your website complies with the General Data Protection Regulation (GDPR) if you're dealing with European customers, or the California Consumer Privacy Act (CCPA) if you're engaging with Californians. These laws provide guidelines on how to handle the personal data of your users.

Intellectual Property Rights

As you build your dropshipping business, protect your brand through trademarks and copyright law. This guards against potential infringement and establishes your business's visual and textual identity. Moreover, be aware of the intellectual property rights of others to avoid legal complications from selling counterfeit or unlicensed merchandise.

Contracts and Documentation

- **Terms of Service:** This is the legal agreement between your business and your customers. It outlines the rules and guidelines that users must agree to in order to use your website and services.

- **Privacy Policy:** This document informs users about the types of personal information your business collects and how that information is used, stored, and protected.

- **Return Policy:** Clear return policies are necessary to maintain customer satisfaction and outline the procedures for managing returns and refunds.

Tackling Tax Obligations

Taxes can be complex, especially with the added dimension of online sales across state lines. Familiarize yourself with your tax obligations, including sales tax, income tax, and any other relevant business taxes. Use accounting software or consult with a tax professional to stay organized and compliant.

Conclusion

It's incumbent upon you as an online entrepreneur to ensure your business operates within the bounds of the law. Diligence in handling the legal aspects of your dropshipping business not only solidifies the foundation for present operations but also paves the way for a robust and scalable future. Consult with legal professionals as necessary to tailor your legal documentation to your specific business needs.

Appendix C: Case Studies and Success Stories

Exploring the triumphs of others can be an excellent catalyst for your own success. We've gathered engrossing case studies and inspiring success stories from entrepreneurs who have carved out their own corner of the digital market. These narratives not only embody the lessons outlined in prior chapters but also offer concrete examples of the diverse paths that can lead to prosperity in online dropshipping.

Lisa's Home Decor Haven

Meet Lisa. Formerly an interior designer, Lisa leveraged her eye for aesthetics to create an online home decor store. She identified her niche after noticing a gap in the market for affordable yet chic home accessories. Focusing on relationships with suppliers known for quality and reliability, she curated a selection that appealed to minimalists who loved modern design. Lisa's story underscores the importance of identifying a profitable niche and harnessing her own expertise to meet customer demands.

Jason's Gadget Garage

Jason's journey began with a passion for the latest tech gadgets. By analyzing market trends and focusing on emerging products, he positioned his online store at the forefront of innovation. Jason's agile approach to inventory management allowed him to pivot quickly with tech trends, always keeping his product selection fresh and appealing.

His success story is a testament to the power of responsiveness in product selection and the significance of being a market trendsetter.

Karen's Fashion Fix

Karen's rise in the online fashion world is a tale of branding mastery. With a keen sense for social media marketing, Karen built a fashion dropshipping business that connected with her audience on a personal level. Her consistent brand messaging across platforms carved a unique identity for her store, helping to garner a loyal customer base. Karen's story illustrates the crucial role comprehensive branding plays in creating a recognizable and trusted online presence.

Mark & Angela's Adventure Gear Outlet

What started as a blogging platform for travel enthusiasts, Mark and Angela's website turned into an adventure gear outlet, featuring products curated through their expeditions. Streamlining order fulfillment was key in their growth, as they needed to keep up with the demand without holding inventory. Their success is a clear example that you can turn a passion into a profitable dropshipping business while emphasizing efficient operational practices.

The Conscious Consumer

This environmentally focused store began as a small project by a group of eco-conscious friends and has grown into a substantial online destination for sustainable goods. Through effective use of SEO and content marketing, they drew in customers who shared their values, and their commitment to excellent customer service fostered a community of repeat buyers. This story is reflective of how businesses with core values can connect with like-minded customers and thrive.

Each of these entrepreneurs started where you are now and achieved success through a combination of savvy planning, sharp marketing, and relentless dedication. Delving into these experiences grants you not just strategies and tips, but also a dose of inspiration to fuel your journey from nascent entrepreneur to dropshipping dynamo. For more information, feel free to visit us at www.MyMaverickWorld.com

www.ingramcontent.com/pod-product-compliance
Lightning Source LLC
Chambersburg PA
CBHW022057170526
45157CB00004B/1383